W9-AVO-221

TEACHING LIFE

TEACHING LIFE

Letters from a Life in Literature

BY DALE SALWAK

University of Iowa Press

Iowa City

▼

University of Iowa Press, Iowa City 52242
Copyright © 2008 by Dale Salwak
www.uiowapress.org
All rights reserved
Printed in the United States of America

Design by Omega Clay

No part of this book may be reproduced or used in any form or by any means without permission in writing from the publisher. All reasonable steps have been taken to contact copyright holders of material used in this book. The publisher would be pleased to make suitable arrangements with any whom it has not been possible to reach.

The University of Iowa Press is a member of Green Press Initiative
and is committed to preserving natural resources.

Printed on acid-free paper

LCCN: 2007940203
ISBN-13: 978-1-58729-630-7
ISBN-10: 1-58729-630-6

08 09 10 11 12 C 5 4 3 2 1

To the memory of my father
STANLEY F. SALWAK
1920–2005
remembered with
gratitude and love

CONTENTS

"No one ever told me that grief felt so like fear." Like an anthem, my memory of C. S. Lewis's words—written on the occasion of his wife's death from cancer—swept over me in 1978 as I sat four rows back, aisle seat, at the funeral for twenty-year-old Kelly (as I will call her), one of my students.

No one is exempt from this fear. I could read it in the faces of her friends as well as her grandparents (who had flown from England to attend), and I could hear it in the concluding words that her mother spoke that morning with eyes deeply, darkly sad: "Kelly brought so much joy and light to our lives. We will go on, of course, but I fear for the future."

Bright, blossoming, full of life—anyone who knew Kelly saw in her the promise of great things. Her death felt all the more poignant for me because, when her Volkswagen was hit broadside by a van, killing her instantly, I was waiting in my office for her to arrive for an appointment.

And so, there I sat, along with several hundred others, stunned and in mourning—for my student, of course, but also for all of us—listening as the rabbi spoke: "When we think about the death and burial of a loved one, we are also contemplating the meaning of death for ourselves. Kelly's short life was richly lived, not wasted. Too many people measure a life by its years rather than by its depth. We think of the short span of our own years, and we want to live them worthily, dynamically, and courageously. Her death—and our contemplation of it—drives us to live more deeply. Death is part of our total experience. It is not separate from life."

I was deeply moved by the traditions that the family followed to involve them in the reality of Kelly's physical loss; and at the gravesite, I was privileged to help with the burial. The sharp grating sound as the point of my shovel sank into the hard earth, then the dull thud as the clump of dirt hit the coffin's lid—all this was blunt, brutal, direct, helping me to absorb the reality of the moment, jolting my heart—exactly as it was intended to do. This was not a movie or a television show. This was not a game. This was real: someone was being placed in the ground and would not return.

At her parents' home the family sat shiva (literally, "seven," for the traditional seven days of mourning) as various rites were observed. An uncle sat on a stool, symbolizing how low he had been brought by grief. Two cousins tore their shirts as a visible manifestation of sorrow, the rips in the fabric paralleling a universe rent by loss. And mirrors of the household had been covered because they symbolized inappropriate vanity at such a sad time. "We don't want to look at our faces," said one mourner. "This reminds us that we have been diminished because one image of God, an image like ourselves, is gone."

Gone, and yet for many weeks afterward, the image of Kelly lingered in my mind. Perhaps it was the suddenness of her death, the utter loss of so much potential, the appointment we never kept, which left me wondering whether anything I had said in class had made a difference in her too-short life—or, for that matter, in the lives of any of my students.

It was a full five years later before I realized that one way to find answers to these slippery questions and many others was to write a series of imagined letters to Kelly (now in my mind a metaphor for all of my students) as if she had survived the accident, completed her undergraduate degree, and gone on to graduate studies in English; as if she had lived a full life—become a teacher herself and earned tenure, published, wondered how to mix marriage and career, faced the death of her father, and much more. Thus was conceived the epistolary memoir that follows.

I hope that college and university students who aspire to enter the teaching profession, as well as educators early in their careers, will benefit from what I have written, but I also have in mind the general reading public for whom I seek to make the contemporary classroom experience with literature better understood and more warmly appreciated. By turns analytical, reflective, and exhortatory, I would like to capture for some readers and awaken in others the fascination, the enlightenment, and the sheer joy that literary studies can offer both the professor and the students. I also want to speak to Western society's prevailing and, for many of us, disturbing prejudice against this noble profession.

In letters, we often clarify our own thinking as we write, shaping the message in a special way for the eyes of the individual reader. With letters, too, we may honor memory. "Letters," says the poet John Donne, "mingle souls." This book mingles my soul with those of Kelly and all the students she has come to symbolize for me.

CHAPTER 1

Transition

Dear Kelly,

Of the many reference letters that I've been privileged to write for aspiring teachers, few have given me greater pleasure than yours. I remember them as easy to compose because in every respect you impressed me as a young woman of real ability. As I said at the time, your value lies in your steady enthusiasm over the long haul, your constant curiosity and dedication to scholarship, your ability and desire to learn, and your general aptitude for the profession. I was not surprised, therefore, when you landed a full-time teaching position, nor will I be surprised a few years from now to hear that you have earned tenure.

To advance in this profession, as you know, requires not only hard work, dedication, excellence in your field, and care for your students but also the support and encouragement of your peers. In many ways academia is a special, closed world with myriad unstated rituals and customs and rules. To learn to work within the system you must learn to connect meaningfully with your colleagues—not only on your campus but generally throughout the academic world. Here are some ideas that, I hope, will help you to do just that.

If you are like most beginning teachers, then the transition from *feeling* like a student to *living* fully as a scholar-teacher will be a challenge. Despite the profound pleasure and gratitude with which I assumed my teaching tasks in 1973 and the generosity with which colleagues greeted me, at least three years passed before I began to feel at ease—perhaps because I was the youngest on campus and the least experienced; perhaps, too, because at the time I was still wearing two hats, one as a teacher in the morning hours, another as a graduate student in the afternoon and evening hours. After so many years as an underling, suddenly I was admitted to the elite ranks of a profession in which, irrespective of age or experience, a certain democratic familiarity prevails. Now those whom I had formerly addressed as "professor" or "doctor" were my peers on a first-name basis. Noting that outside of the classroom I didn't talk much, one colleague called me "secretive." It wasn't that at all. I was watch-fully self-aware of what I said to others, and when and how, because I didn't want to offend and because I wanted to learn. I absorbed everything.

"Resisting reality is a fruitless endeavor," says Emerson. When you are feeling uncomfortable, remind yourself to live fully in the present, your new present, just as you had learned to do for years as a student. Here I find Joshua 1:8 is helpful: "Do not turn from [the law] to the right or to the left, so that you may have success wherever you go." Deviating to the right is extreme rationalism; to the left, extreme emotionalism. Do not make them your criteria for behavior or decisions. If you postpone your work until you are secure, your work will never begin. If you put off your pursuit of knowledge for a suitable moment, that moment will never come. If you delay a task until conditions are favorable, favorable conditions will never arise. Instead, stay focused on the reasons you were hired: to study and to disseminate from your field the best that is known and thought and discovered in the world. Everything else—including personnel conflicts, academic politics, or lingering insecurities (of which there will be many)—is secondary to your work.

While difficult to fall back on in some circumstances, keeping the work paramount has many practical applications in your relation-ship to others nonetheless. Someone has spoken ill of you? Overlook or confront that person, if you must, clear the air, and return to the novel you were reading—or writing. You feel resentful about an ad-ministrative decision? Express your point of view, ask questions un-til you understand the context, and then go back to grading essays. Your application for a grant or a promotion is turned down? Talk it over with an expert, resolve to do better the next time, and then pre-pare tomorrow's lecture. Although we can't always control our cir-cumstances, we can control our reactions to those circumstances.

No matter how balanced you try to be, you will have moments of pettiness and crankiness, irritation and anger. By staying focused on your work rather than on personality differences, Kelly, you'll find it easier to live graciously, to be tactful to everyone, and to avoid petty faculty disputes or temporary ill will. You'll also honor your colleagues' dignity by resisting gossip whenever possible and avoiding malicious conversations. If you can do all that, then people will take you into their confidence—a high compliment indeed. Never betray that trust, but be sure your intimates are tested, and try not to say anything about anyone that you wouldn't be willing to share with that person twenty-four hours later. (The Earl of Chesterfield's advice to his son, Philip, applies here, too: "You should never put in a letter something you would not want read out in open court.")

The problem with speaking unkind words is that they may reflect how we feel the day we speak them, but they are never our last words on any subject, nor are they a settled view. We move on, our passions cool, our attitude changes, but the hearer of our words might ruminate upon them and fan them into a story that can easily spread to others and be misinterpreted or taken out of context. I've seen more than one career ruined when a disaffected teacher barely out of the gate tried to dominate faculty and departmental meetings by forcing curriculum changes, insulting the administration on every score, and complaining about everything under the sun. His bravado masked a deep-rooted insecurity that alienated him from his peers, his students, and ultimately his campus.

I've also seen how the power of work can transform an individual from suspicious to trustworthy. On one occasion a new teacher arrived on my campus driven by the idea that academic life is competitive, a perpetual struggle to survive. At times she said she imagined herself surrounded and outnumbered by people who resented her for being different from them. She displayed defensiveness in a setting within which she felt herself, at best, only tolerated; on a campus where she was often suspected of being snobbish, she felt she had to prove continually that she was not. These experiences carried over into staff meetings, giving her the habit of identifying with a threatened minority. If there was disagreement over placement exams or research papers or committee assignments, you could bet she'd always oppose the departmental view. I watched as her emotion got astride of reason, invective displaced argument, and suspicion eroded trust.

But once she locked into her passion for her discipline and became fully engaged in both her work with students and her research projects, her insecurities disappeared, her belligerence subsided, and she endeared herself to most of the staff and faculty. Paying attention to her work, she discovered, is an effective antidote for doubts, egotism, and self-consciousness.

Connecting with others does not mean abdicating your self or losing the integrity of your mind. In the unlikely event that you are invited to do something unethical, for example, remember that you're never so beholden that you can't walk away from it and start over. At no time allow yourself to need a job so much that you're willing to compromise on your principles to attain or keep it. "Saying no to others," writes Cheryl Jarvis, "is saying yes to something deeper within ourselves."

Once after I had applied for an administrative post, a colleague offered to slip me a copy of the questions I would be asked at the interview, on the premise that "another of the applicants already has them." Of course I said "no"—emphatically—and explained that I'd prefer to see how I performed in the interview unaided. Did he so underestimate my intelligence that he thought, even for a moment, that I might accept the offer? Or was he testing my integrity? Either way, I resented his offer, but I chose to say nothing more and quietly withdrew my name from the pool of applicants. If I had allowed those negative feelings to fester, however, then my work would have suffered and eventually I might have said something to him that I would later regret. I had to depersonalize the event and move on with my duties as if it had never happened. Neither the job nor the fleeting satisfaction of venting my dismay was worth the price of compromising my better judgment.

Such experiences are the exception. In most instances faculty members are drawn together as colleagues in a genuine spirit of camaraderie and cooperation, and our work becomes the great leveler.

What a pleasure it is to sit down with experts from disciplines as diverse as physics and psychology, economics and the arts and discover how much we share in common. Do you recall the exchange in *Persuasion* between Anne and her cousin Mr. Elliot?

> "My idea of good company, Mr. Elliot, is the company of well-informed people, who have a great deal of conversation; that is what I call good company."
> "You are mistaken," he said gently. "That is not good company, that is the best."

Occasionally adversarial and contentious, more often civil and generous, these searching conversations help to orient us to the wide contours of the world and give us a balanced perspective that our own education may have neglected. The expertise of our colleagues and the open exchange of ideas enrich us in ways that we'll perhaps never fully comprehend.

Sometimes unwittingly we even become a testing ground for a classroom idea. One day I had just sat down in the cafeteria to eat when a student approached my table and asked me to watch her books and purse while she got lunch. No sooner had she left than a young man ran past the table, grabbed the purse, and bolted out the door. Just as quickly I sprang from my seat and ran after him. Outside, I was greeted by a crowd of students, applauding, along with the culprit and the "victim," holding her purse. I realized that a colleague of mine and his psychology class had brilliantly set me up in a group experiment. I had fallen into their trap, but I had passed.

That episode, and others, encouraged me to visit classrooms to see some of my colleagues at work. Listening to and watching them provides us with the pleasure and opportunity to learn how our peers connect with the students, how they overcome the challenges of a different group—in short, how they "sell" themselves and their material. Although we may know what's coming, the students don't, and watching the teacher gauge and work with that suspense not only gives me great satisfaction but expands my own pedagogical repertoire.

Although collegiality is a great gift, so, too, is diversity of views.

As you know, many colleagues will hold different values and beliefs and interests from yours, and although at times their opposition may make you feel uncomfortable, well-managed, reasonable conflict can have a very positive outcome. We have a lot to learn from those who think differently from us. It helps us to better understand our own ideas. After all, didn't F. Scott Fitzgerald say that the mark of an educated person is the ability to hold two opposing ideas in mind simultaneously and not be paralyzed by them? Strip everything away, and a college campus is the center of careful, reflective, divergent thought—and the synergy that arises from the interchange of views can be stimulating.

For more than thirty years one professor was an insistently hovering presence on our campus. A tough teacher, he demanded and received dedication from all of his students. For his pedagogy I admired him greatly and adopted some of his techniques, but in philosophy and politics we were wide apart. It's not an exaggeration to say that I could easily predict his position on almost any issue—for it would be the opposite of mine. Neither of us set out to convert the other to his way of thinking. Neither of us was deliberately pernicious or contentious. Each of us understood that a teacher needs opposition as much as praise to maintain the vitality of his or her craft. We both enjoyed intellectual combat, and I learned a great deal from him.

You'll also learn a great deal from serving on committees. This experience will season you, broaden your understanding of how your institution operates, and give you a role in determining its future. I'm always impressed by how generously many teachers give of their time and effort without reward and with little recognition. Look at the proliferation of committees on any campus—from accreditation studies to scholarships to curriculum—and you'll find many dedicated teachers working tirelessly alongside administrators to chart the course of their college.

I encourage and admire committee service; it's one of our duties, but be careful to avoid what Jacques Barzun calls the "professional disease." This occurs when teachers, having completed a morning's classes, feels they must do something that counts as more work.

Inspiration for writing or reading doesn't come, no students show up during office hours, and so, conscience-stricken, they feel they must attend a meeting. Over time, this leads to another and then another until eventually they become addicted to frenzied professional activities—and find themselves caught up in a race against time with no time for their own work. The novel remains unwritten. The dissertation lies incomplete. The class preps begin to suffer. My advice is to search for a balance between detachment and involvement. Choose wisely, contribute as you must; but sometimes, it's important and ethical to say "no." (One of the compensations of growing older is that you can say "no" without feeling guilty.) Don't allow yourself to be overwhelmed by minutiae, and never lose sight of the main reason you're on campus. Successful teachers are known by the mark they leave on their students.

By advising you to monitor your collegial services, I'm not suggesting that you seal yourself off from your supervisors. Get to know them as the professionals they are, and you'll discover what useful resources they can be. Many come from extensive teaching backgrounds themselves and are eager to share with you their experiences if you will pepper them with questions about their classes, their research, their successes and disappointments. It's not a bad idea to present yourself to the president and ask how you can contribute; other faculty and administrators can help you clarify questions, address issues, explore opportunities for professional development, and serve your students and your institution more effectively.

Despite what you will hear from some, administration is neither the enemy nor a foreign body irritating the faculty's eye. Neither of us has much force without the other, and our dependence on each other and on our students is fundamental to the very definition of the academic enterprise. Every hired faculty member represents a potential investment of thirty to forty years or more; for that reason alone the selection, development, and advancement process is complex and slow. You are in your position because certain individuals believed in you. Having proved yourself as a student, now you must prove yourself to your employers, and one way of furthering that cause is by making yourself known to, and getting to know, them.

Perhaps because I've seen academic life from both camps for so long (my father was a university president for twelve years, and before that he held other administrative positions, including assistant to the provost at the University of Massachusetts), I've always had an instinctive appreciation for the fragile bond of mutual trust and friendliness that must exist between faculty and administrators if an educational institution is to function smoothly. Some grievances (from either side) are warranted, I'm sure, but the vast majority of cases of hostilities or distrust strike me as unnecessary, harmful, and self-serving. I once heard that an incoming president at another institution had asked faculty members, one by one, to justify what they were teaching. This struck me as a perfectly fair question and a wonderful opportunity for faculty to rethink course objectives. But you'd be amazed at the uproar it created, with many expressing outrage at the perceived insult, threatening lawsuits, and in two cases even resigning from their positions to go elsewhere.

On a smaller scale, when I began teaching a new course, Literature of the Bible, my first semester's enrollment was at a low of fifteen students and the dean wanted to cancel the class outright. I could have allowed myself to feel threatened, but I wanted to understand his point of view and said so. I also said, "Give me another semester, and I'll fill the class." I then went to work to promote it, and it has exceeded its cap since then. By working together with a larger goal in mind, the dean and I were able to enhance learning opportunities for our students.

From all I've said I don't mean to suggest that campus life is always sober and rigorously intellectual. Along with patience, tact, tolerance, and respect, your success within the community of teachers also depends on the capacity to be amused. Many of my colleagues love practical jokes, and many of us love to play them.

Early in my career I shared an eighteen-square-foot office with David. Most of the space was taken up by two large wooden desks, set facing each other. Unknown to me at the time, each week he pushed his desk forward a half-inch and mine back a half-inch. This went on for months without arousing my suspicions until one day, when I tried to open my drawer, my elbow hit the back wall. I do remember thinking it odd how cramped I felt while at the opposite end David sat comfortably chatting with two of his students. The next day, after a good laugh, I returned the desks to their original positions with a line drawn on the wall and two arrows, pointing in opposite directions. But revenge was to be mine.

One June day we were quite tired from grading final exams. The outer door opened and in walked one of his students. When I whispered this to David he said, "Please, just tell her I'm not in," and then he hid under his desk. When the student asked "Is Dr. S. in?" I pointed and said, "Yes, he's under his desk." Instantly, David pulled himself out and stood up, face beet red, holding a paper clip and said, "Here it is!" He always was a quick thinker.

Sometimes, humor arises out of our relations with students. I'm thinking here of the late Bernard Zavidowsky, whom I had the privilege of knowing as a colleague and friend from 1973 until his death in 1999. One of his persistent complaints was that students misspelled his last name, or mispronounced it. *This* was an opportunity I couldn't let pass.

And so, on several occasions, I left an unsigned, handwritten note taped to his door. "Dear Mr. Zavidoosky," I wrote one time. "I need to see you right away about my essay. When can we meet?" Then I waited for him to discover it, sitting quietly in my adjoining office and listening through the open door to expressions of disbelief, followed by the sound of crumpling paper and then a dull thud as the note hit the bottom of his wastepaper basket.

Of course, we who are inclined to turn to humor in our interactions must not overdo it, or we might suffer what the poet Philip Larkin calls the "familiar humorist's fate" of not being taken seriously at all. There is a time and a place for laughter, as there is for more serious interchanges. A pinch of spice—not a handful—makes the flavor piquant.

Finally, few of us climb the academic ladder toward tenure and beyond without the assistance and encouragement and mentoring of others. I owe a lot to my department chair, Patricia Barney, who was sympathetic, patient, and fully human when it was most needed; to a vice president and three colleagues in particular who made the time in their overcrowded schedules to teach me the ropes; and to our president, Robert D. Haugh, who believed in my abilities before I had given much evidence of them. Memories of how well I was treated when I began my career have stayed with me throughout the years and now influence the way I myself try to encourage and work with incoming faculty.

Often I reflect on the circumstances surrounding my own job search. Although there were few openings in 1972, and although I had heard many stories of frustrated job-seekers, I began in the fall by writing ten letters a day for twenty-two days to every college and university English department in five western states. All but three responded with regrets; two offered interviews (which I gave); and another said that although no opening was available, they'd keep my name on file. Three months later, a letter arrived to say that they now had a vacancy.

I suppose we find what we expect to find. I wanted an academic home where I would have the freedom to grow as a teacher and a scholar; where I would be surrounded by a supportive faculty and staff who are themselves growing intellectually; where I could work with challenging students, eager to learn about the books that matter and the authors I've met. I found all that, and much more, here at Citrus College. I wish the same for you.

I'll never know what went through the minds of the selection committee the morning they read my application, or the thoughts of the president as he reviewed the applications the night before scheduling interviews, or what was said after I'd completed the forty-five-minute interview and left the room. But what I do know is that six weeks later the phone rang and my whole life changed; and that I'll be forever grateful that I was selected; and that it's my obligation and responsibility to do my very best, every day, and to treat my fellow workers and my students as I would like to be treated.

I also know that you, Kelly, prize real teaching and fine writing and good books and genuine people. You have no time for their opposites. Your life and gifts are too precious to be squandered.

I know, too, that if you stay focused on the *essential you*, if you remember the reasons you applied and were subsequently hired, and if you commit to living peacefully and respectfully with your col-leagues, then you'll not only lessen many of the tensions and anxi-eties inherent in the job, but also contribute more and enjoy the journey, too.

And I know that thirty-five years from now you'll look back, as I often do, and be able to say honestly that, despite years of sometimes seemingly overwhelming effort, frequent worry, complicated deal-ings with complex personalities, and even despair, it was all worth it because you served a cause greater than yourself, a cause rooted in your work—work that has touched literally thousands of lives. For I'm sure that you, too, will write many letters of recommendation for students on the threshold of becoming colleagues. And thus the challenging and glorious cycle continues.

Warm regards,

CHAPTER 2

Epiphanies

Dear Kelly,

I read with interest your answer to my question, "What do I 're-ally' need to know about teaching?" Certainly there are challenges enough in a profession that demands so much from the hearts and minds of its practitioners. While I agree that "grading through the stacks of essays" and "staying current in the field" and "finding the energy to stay fresh at the podium" are challenges, they seem self-evident when compared with what I had in mind—and that is convincing our students that what they are studying applies to their lives in purposeful and meaningful ways.

I think you'll agree that there was a time in school when we silently questioned the relevance of some of our courses. What persuaded us otherwise? Apart from earning a good grade or fulfilling qualifications for a degree, do you recall anyone (other than our parents) explaining *why* we must know something? I certainly don't. Not to be critical, but I suppose most of our teachers expected us to discover reasons on our own, which by some miracle we did. And so, there came a particular point in my life when I shed my indifference to some subjects and, like you, discovered a deep hunger to learn whatever I could from any topic I encountered. From that moment, I became a student and realized my calling.

Kelly, the opportunity for these precious moments is available to everyone who enters a classroom, but only if he or she is prepared and able to receive them. That's where you, the teacher, fit in. Remember what Emerson proposes: "The whole secret of the teacher's force lies in the conviction that men [and women] are convertible, and they are."

To prepare your students to be open to such moments, it's important to set your posture, to create an atmosphere conducive to intellectual inquiry and expansion. First impressions are all important. From the syllabus your students should know instantly how much you care about the subject and how important it is that each of them is there to learn. I believe that most students are contemptuous of triviality. They expect and hope for serious, competent discussions of assigned texts, and they want to be challenged to think deeply. I would be nervous to enter the classroom before I had learned as much as I could about the course material and spent lots of time and energy contemplating what would be most beneficial for them to learn.

A syllabus is more than a chronological listing of assignments. It is a covenant of trust between you and the student, and a covenant is only as strong as the integrity of the person making it. See that yours is professional in all respects and developed with the same careful attention to detail that you would give to a book proposal before sending it to a publisher. It should be well organized, with clearly stated objectives and requirements and a bibliography of recommended supplementary readings from which you intend to draw during the semester. At the end of your syllabus, you might want to include this paragraph:

> If you aren't here to work exceptionally hard and at the same time have what I hope will be an enjoyable semester, then please drop now so that I can give the seat to someone who needs the class and who is serious about doing well. All of us have long wait lists, and we would like to enroll students who intend to stay in class for its duration and do their very best. I am interested in having a core of students who fit into that category. We have fifty-four hours together—let's not waste them.

These words may strike you as a bit harsh, yet I find they have the intended effect of awakening students (if they need awakening) to my expectations and assuring them of the importance of time—theirs and mine. Like you, I want my students to be fully alive to the present, to take every advantage of every opportunity presented to them, and to celebrate the fact that they have the greatest gift, an inquiring mind, and the liberty to think for themselves. Nothing could be worse for a student than to conclude a formal education and think, "Ah, the student I might have been!"—and then to spend the rest of life explaining why he or she didn't do better.

Along with clearly communicated expectations, convey your excitement, and in so doing ignite theirs. What did St. Augustine say? "One loving spirit sets another on fire." Enthusiasm is contagious; if you care passionately about your subject, your students can't help but listen. You should get a genuine thrill out of offering the material each day; if you don't, you should examine your thoughts and preparation. Perhaps you don't yet believe in its importance or you just haven't found a way to share or express your passion for learning. You say that you chose this level of teaching because college was your favorite time in school. Well, work to make it *their* favorite time, too. One day when he was fifteen years old my son, Ryan, said suddenly, "Isn't it exciting to discover something new!" Exactly so. Each day in class should be like that, for you and for your students as well. Catch the romance of discovery. Create expectancy. *Hold nothing back*. Your job is to make the written word come alive.

I am unsurprised to hear that some of your students don't share your consuming passion for literature, but you can help them to do so by relating your world to theirs. History was not among my strong subjects early in high school—perhaps in part because of uninspired teaching or, more likely, my own ignorance and immaturity and fear. But when a teacher set one of my favorite novels, Hawthorne's *The Scarlet Letter*, into its historical context, Puritan America came alive for me—the era exploded with meaning, and my mind opened to possibilities I might never have known otherwise. It was a fateful discovery. From that day, I've never stopped reading history because the more I learn about its course and its people, the more I learn about the literature I love.

You can also help to ignite students' passion by meeting them at their point of need. This means walking into the classroom with the assumption that in a corner of their lives some of them are burdened or lost. You can infer this from their expressions or body language, their tone of voice, or their written answers to questions about interests and background. Some are lonely; others suffer from a lack of direction; still others are confused about meaning or what they perceive to be an absence of meaning. Others are teetering between confusion and clarity, between doubt and assurance. A few are anxious about measuring up to the college's standards. Many are not even sure whether they should be there. Don't ask them to explain. Maybe those are spirits they must grapple with as a necessary part of growing, maturing, and functioning in an often baffling world. What you can do through the readings as well as stories from your life, however, is offer encouragement that others, too, have felt the call of something deeper within, and that the best way they can prepare themselves to respond is by plunging into the sea of ideas and information surrounding them.

No person can truly develop in this life without receiving the understanding of at least one other person. When we care for others, we always strive to become better than we are; and when we strive to become better than we are, everything around us becomes better, too. Like most of your colleagues, I know that you care about what your students think. I know that you solicit their first impressions, feelings, and reactions to a piece of literature as a way of encouraging them to teach themselves. And I know that you believe, as I do, that they are in your classes not by coincidence or by accident—but by design. Trust your place in this and look for—make space for—the moments that confirm it.

I'm reminded of one student whose letter to me illustrates my point. "I'd just like to add that your class came at a good time for me," she wrote.

By this, I mean, I was ready for it. Your class was often a lot like a type of therapy for me. It was always positive, even when what we were reading was dark. As a recent single parent of three children (ages twelve, nine, and two), dealing with that, with death, with loss, sickness and with other issues which are a part of life, I often found unexpected comfort in your discussions as well as the literature. I cannot possibly ever thank you enough for that; it has made a big difference.

Personal stories can penetrate powerfully into the lives of your students, especially those who can't be swayed by abstract reasoning or persuasion. Remember what Jacques Barzun said of Emerson, perhaps America's greatest proponent of the rational: arguments convince nobody. "But when something is merely said or—better yet, hinted at," Burzun said, "there is a kind of hospitality in our imagination. We are ready to accept it." Kelly, the material you present will suggest answers to students' questions, and they will listen and respond as if the message were for them.

One student from my Children's Literature class, for instance, wrote that she was especially affected by a class discussion of *Peter Pan* when I had summarized the consequences of "shadowy figures" (masculine/father and feminine/mother roles) in a child's life. "As I write, tears fill my eyes," she began.

> For me, both of my parents were shadowy to nonexistent. My father was absent; I never knew him. As a youngster I hated this person that I did not know because of the guilt I was made to feel by some family members for his invisibility. You were correct in your statement, "Children should not be put into the position of bearing the guilt placed upon them by the actions of irresponsible adults." This was my "epiphany" moment! My grandmother's voice in my head many years after her demise kept reminding me, "You should not hate—it will destroy you. You can't move forward until you stop looking back." Your lecture released me from the guilt. I am now aware of my destiny. Like Barrie and so many other authors we covered this semester, I shall write about my experience and lecture young men and women about the consequences to the child of being born out of wedlock.

We never know the effect a reading assignment or subsequent discussion might have upon a student, do we? A teacher of literature has hundreds of classic examples to choose from, of course, but on the first day—regardless of the class—I like to plunge into the first twenty-five lines from Canto I of Dante's *The Divine Comedy* because they speak lastingly on a topic that everyone cares about.

As Dante brilliantly describes, there came a time midway in his life when he awakened to know that he was lost, and that all his goals were empty and meaningless. He calls this moral uncertainty a "dark wood of error" and a moment of great fear, "so bitter it goes nigh to death." He doesn't know how he got there, but as he implies, the moment that he knew he was lost was the start of finding his way.

In that knowledge the poet looks up and sees the first rays of dawn (or divine illumination) on the shoulder of a little hill. Naturally, he yearns for that light and so he races toward it. But his action is foolish and childlike. Three beasts block his way, together symbolizing the worldly ambition that stands between where he is and where he wants to be.

Later in the text, we follow the poet on his perilous journey from error to truth, from darkness to light as he learns to renounce his self-centeredness, face up to and overcome the perversities at the core of his soul, and embrace wholeness. As Dante discovers, and as most great literature, music, art, and philosophy confirm, nothing is harder or more important in the whole human condition than achieving a full sense of who we are, where we are going, what we mean to live and die for. For the rest of his life Dante never loses sight of the depth from which he had been lifted.

Now you might say, "Well, this would never work for me. I can't expect my students to be acquainted with the fourteenth century. Too many of them don't even like poetry. How will they ever manage the archaic words and vague allusions? They're not even Italian!" Yes, that may be true, but in education the things that matter most seldom come easily. They'll work to understand *anything* if it's important to them. The objections you list are easily overcome by talking about the good of the poem, by relating it to their lives, and by explaining how it has benefited or affected your own. Nobody can refute personal experience.

Also, encourage your students to imagine themselves as Dante (or any author or painter or mathematician or whomever you happen to be studying). What would it be like to be him? Ask students to think about how they would feel if they adopted his beliefs. Most important, suggest that they explore what qualities of him they might find in themselves. In other words, encourage them to come to the work on the author's terms and allow themselves to be drawn into his or her world as if they were born to it. At the same time, emphasize that to fully experience literature—or for that matter history, sociology, anthropology, psychology—we must rid ourselves of the notion that we are studying people far removed from us by time, place, or culture. There's no such separation. People did not live in the past; they lived in the present, *their* present. Dante was living in his *present*. Granted, it was a present different from our own, but it was filled with people very much like us and with problems and challenges very much like our own.

Hence, as you well know, the differences between one age and another are superficial; the similarities are deep and enduring. And revealing: in matters of the heart, human nature has not changed in six thousand years of recorded civilization. We share with our predecessors identical needs, desires, fears, and potential for good or, alas, evil. Even the most confident and talented individuals have known bitter and lonely hours. Even the strongest suffered pain, both physical and emotional. Even the most loyal knew betrayal. Only through great struggle does any human being grow in body and mind and spirit. C. S. Lewis calls this the doctrine of "the Unchanging Human Heart," and my belief in it underscores much of what I say in the classroom.

This commonality can be oddly reassuring, especially to students—who are often immersed in examining various belief systems and engaged in deconstructing and reconstructing their own. As burdensome as our problems seem to us, we can be sure that others before us suffered through the same. You have no doubt discovered for yourself that the better we understand the struggles and triumphs and defeats of those who preceded us, the better we understand ourselves. If you can help your students to connect with truths such as this one, Kelly, then you will have reached their hearts; and by reaching their hearts, you will engage their minds; and by awakening both, you will set them well on their journey toward discovery.

Ultimately, every one of our classes in the curriculum should invite students to examine themselves; or in the words of Thoreau, to "live deliberately, to front only the essential facts of life." In Eudora

Welty's words, "All serious daring begins within"—but to dare takes great courage and conviction.

When I was in high school, T. S. Eliot's "The Love Song of J. Alfred Prufrock" was expected reading of everyone in sophomore English not only for its importance to literary history but because, as my teacher said, "It presents the opposite of what we would wish for our own lives." Prufrock, as you know, doesn't dare to act. He is torn between a desire to change and a fear to change, between recognizing how unhappy he is and burying himself in the triviality of polite society. He has abdicated his will. Through him, Eliot has much to say about the hollowness of modern society and the decay of culture in modern Western civilization.

Now, if you were to ask how many college students have read it, perhaps at most a half-dozen would raise their hands; and if you were to ask why the others haven't, their answer would be because it wasn't assigned. Why wasn't it assigned? The common explanation is that students can't relate to it—a very useful excuse applied to a lot of serious literature, but one that I abandoned long ago as being untrue.

No, I believe "Prufrock" is avoided because students *can* relate to it; that is, if one takes the time to read and discuss it carefully, then the truths it conveys hit too close to home—perhaps in the teacher, perhaps in some of the students who are living half-lives without ever knowing it, perhaps in the administrators setting the curriculum. You could make the same argument for a host of readings that you and I took for granted when we were in school, from Shakespeare to William Blake to Emily Dickinson.

This neglect ought to make us both sad and angry. As one of my students put it: "I had never felt as though I was being cheated of something when I was in high school, so why do I feel that way now? What was the reasoning behind some of my former teachers' thoughts?"

Cheated is the accurate word here. Some students come to us woefully underprepared in the great works of literature, philosophy, history, and the fine arts. This is not their fault. They have been raised in a digital, visual culture that discourages interiority and by parents who don't talk to their children, don't take them to museums and libraries, don't encourage them to read, and don't ask them thoughtful questions about serious moral and social issues. Everybody is in a hurry, like the mother I overheard one day in a bookstore who was looking for the CliffsNotes to *Great Expectations*:

> "Why do you want them?" the store manager asked.
> "Well, to help my son answer some questions on a take-home examination," she said.
> "Wouldn't you rather have your son read the book and discover the answers for himself?"
> "Well, I don't know."

Jacob Needleman in his book *Time and the Soul* calls this everyday phenomenon "the poverty of our affluence . . . It is the famine of a culture that has chosen . . . the external world over the internal world" because we're too busy or too distracted or, perhaps, too afraid to think for ourselves. But what happens if the television burns out and the computers go off and the malls are closed and friends move away and loved ones die and magazines, newspapers, and sporting events are canceled and parties are discontinued and libraries and school doors are shut and liquor stores and theaters are closed? What then? We are alone with ourselves.

Alone with ourselves: No sooner have I written the words than I think of Sundays as they used to be when I was a child—carefree, unstructured, with all but essential services closed, streets all but empty of cars. Has anyone considered that perhaps one of the reasons Sundays have become ever more crowded with events is because we want to avoid the very purpose for which the day was set aside in the first place—for worship and rest and reflection? If this is true for society in general, why should it be any less true for the classroom, which has become a cross section of society at its best and, sometimes, its worst?

Pascal is right: "If our condition were truly happy we should not need to divert ourselves from thinking about it . . . the sole cause of our unhappiness is that we do not know how to sit quietly in our room." Along with fulfilling the academic objectives of the class, my aim through our readings and discussions is to guide students to a place where they can face the deepest truths about themselves, and see where they lead.

It is in our nature to know. An appetite for knowledge and beauty exists in our minds, writes C. S. Lewis, "and God makes no appetite in vain." Stimulate that appetite in your students, Kelly, and it will revolutionize their lives. I know, because I've seen it happen in many hundreds of my students since I first began to teach in 1973. I saw it happen in you, too.

Warm regards,

CHAPTER 3

Only Connect

Dear Kelly,

You know by now that the secret behind a teacher's (or a student's) growth comes down to one essential word: study—and lots of it. But you also know that it isn't enough merely to understand the material. As one semester leads into another and as the years mount up, slowly the teacher works on the material, until it sinks straight to the bottom of the mind, where it ferments and where everything that comes along later can settle on it. "Conscious learning becomes unconscious knowledge," the surgeon Atul Gawande has written, "and you cannot say precisely how."

We can live privately in a rich confusion of books and manuscripts, always reading and writing, 'til the cows come home (as my grandfather would say), but at some point we must step out of the office or the library and into the classroom—and risk what we have learned. In teaching, as in most professions, skill, judgment, and confidence are learned through experience, a process that is often halting and sometimes humiliating. Slowly, as we develop a strong set of student-listening ears, we revise our approaches, strategies, and attitudes, sometimes ruthlessly. Along the way, we discover how to take unmistakable command of both the material and of those who have arrived to learn. We discover how to connect with our students.

Five years into my career I began to understand how these words applied to my classroom. I was teaching a course in short fiction and the essay, and halfway through my lecture suddenly I realized that I wasn't thinking about myself. I wasn't concerned about finding the precise words to speak. A drape of rapt silence had fallen upon the students, there was a focus and connection such as I'd rarely experienced before, and my full attention was on them and their full attention was on the ideas I was sharing. It was literally a meeting of the minds.

When this communion occurs, we have experienced one of the real joys of our profession. "It is a spiritual contact hardly conscious yet ever renewed," says Dante Gabriel Rossetti, "and which must be a part of the very act of production." Connecting on this level with our students is as much a gift as an instinct, and every teacher has to discover individually how to make it happen. I suspect some never do.

There are all sorts of ways to initiate this connection. Some of my best professors looked us squarely in the eyes, and that conveyed confidence. Or they listened carefully to us as we spoke, and that communicated respect. Or they persuaded us of the truthfulness of their words, and that produced trust. Or they delivered their message in such a way that it seemed as though they were speaking personally to each one of us, and that created a desire to listen. One of my undergraduate teachers was particularly adept at forging that personal link. "It's uncanny," I recall saying one day to a friend as we left class, "but I swear that as I listened to his lecture, it was as if he were speaking just to me." She nodded, and said, "I felt that way, too."

How can we make such a connection with our students? Here's one suggestion: as you walk into a classroom, Kelly, imagine that the person you care most about is seated in the room. It might be a friend, a spouse, a sibling—someone to whom your soul is knit. During your class, take in everyone, of course, but think about that special person and teach to him or her. This imagined audience of one gives you a focus; it puts a human face on your purpose for being there in the first place—to share the joy of learning. If you will do this consistently, then in time you'll find yourself embracing everybody with similar feelings and thoughts, and they in turn will do the same for you. In a corner of your mind this handful of intimates will become and then remain your inner audience. They will help you to stay engaged and motivated; they will inspire you to do your best every day.

In some ways this inner audience is like a muse—the source of creative inspiration and intellectual challenge that artists have laid claim to for centuries. Some teachers, like some authors, can force their muse. But this has never been my way. When, for example, my dean assigned me to teach an Introduction to Shakespeare class, I asked for a year to prepare, for I knew it would take that long to do the kind of job that was expected of me. In doing so, I envisioned myself sitting in class—as an eighteen-year-old student, with a very limited understanding of the playwright's world. Once, we could expect our students to be acquainted with some of the plays, along with the sonnets and the culture; but I knew this was no longer the case and that, although I would be teaching some of the most talented young men and women on campus, I would have to provide that literary and cultural context if they were to understand the plays. I couldn't force this. I had to do my research and trust that my approach, ideas, and voice would emerge in time to take up the assignment.

My preparation included rereading all 38 of Shakespeare's plays, the 154 sonnets, and a half-dozen other poems of varying lengths. I revisited the key critical voices on the subject since the mid-1600s and read the most important books to appear on Shakespeare in the past five years (including Frank Kermode's *Shakespeare's Language*, Marjorie Garber's *Shakespeare After All*, Harold Bloom's *Shakespeare: The Invention of the Human*, and Stephen Greenblatt's *Will in the World*). I subscribed and listened to the Teaching Company's Great Courses series *William Shakespeare: Comedies, Histories, and Tragedies* and *Shakespeare: The Word and the Action* (Peter Saccio, Dartmouth College) as well as *A History of England from the Tudors to the Stuarts* (Robert Bucholz, Loyola University of Chicago). Then after selecting the plays and poems that I wanted to cover in the class, I sketched out ideas for a semester's worth of lectures and discussions, outlining these and refining them over the summer months.

Along with a careful, step-by-step analysis of each play's development, I chose to focus on four key questions that I hoped, together with the students, to answer during the semester: (1) Why is Shakespeare so necessary to our culture? (2) How can we account for the timelessness of Shakespeare? (3) How does Shakespeare help us to understand the Western character and therefore ourselves? (4) How can an achievement of this magnitude be explained? (i.e., How did Shakespeare write *Shakespeare*?)

As in all of my classes, I have found that one of the secrets to bringing the subject alive for the students and engaging their interest daily is to meet them at their points of need. Here, Shakespeare makes it easier for us as teachers because he is always two playwrights—one of his time and one of our time. I like to think of his plays as letters from the dead (Shakespeare) to the living (ourselves). The plays are works of art whose meaning grows and changes as they encounter new imaginations. Most of us attend the theater in search of other selves, so Shakespeare matters because no one else gives us so many selves. As Ben Jonson says, his characters are "rammed with life." We read him because on our own we could never get to know this many people so very profoundly.

When I think back on how thoroughly I had to re-explore Shakespeare before I felt I could help my students explore him, too, I realize that I was responding, unconsciously, to a fundamental question: To whom as teachers are we speaking? The obvious answer, of course, is our students. But we are also speaking to the many voices that have preceded us—the authors we've read, the professors we've studied under, the colleagues we've worked with. As teachers, in other words, we are also in an ongoing "dialogue" with our peers and our predecessors. The better we are acquainted with sympathetic or competing voices in scholarship, the more exuberant and wide-ranging will be our own presentations, and the more closely we will connect with the material and therefore with our students. Every book we teach reaches back to other books—to the books it answers or quotes from or imitates or steals from. We don't begin our careers at the beginning; we start *in medias res*—in the middle of things.

If students can't follow our words, however, or if they aren't given time to digest our presentations, then they won't learn from us. And so I would also like to suggest that you imagine a teaching session to be a series of snapshots and that each student is holding a camera. You've read a passage from a Hemingway novel? Give them time to take a picture with their mind's eye. "Click." You've talked about the dust jacket on a first-edition Faulkner novel? Allow them to push the shutter release. "Ping." You've written on the board a passage from a book? Pause so that they can record it. "Snap." The pace with which you work is determined in part by the size of the class. You lecture and lead a discussion more slowly and more deliberately with a group of three hundred than you do with thirty.

But to connect, you don't always need to speak. Silence, too, can be effective. On occasion, I've awakened too hoarse to talk. I could have chosen to stay home, but my obligation was to my students, so if I felt well enough I went to class and found a way to communicate without speaking. I began by writing on the board: "I have lost my voice. I feel fine." Then I began to "lecture" and lead a discussion by writing the points on the board, asking questions and responding to theirs. With experience, a rhythm develops spontaneously, a rhythm I can't adequately convey in a letter, but one that you'll discover when you try it. Of necessity you'll find yourself eliminating fillers, using only essential words, and communicating directly to your class. To borrow from Hemingway, "You can omit anything you want as long as you know what you've omitted and that you make the reader feel more than he sees."

Another way to connect is to only ask questions. One of my history professors in college used this approach. The second day of the semester we arrived having read a chapter in our text the night before. The professor asked, "Does anyone have any questions about the reading?" No one spoke, and so he said: "Fine, class is over. I'll see you Friday." Friday arrived; we came to class having read another assignment, and once again he asked, "Does anyone have any questions about the reading?" Again, no one spoke, and so again he said, "I'll see you Monday." Well, by now we began to catch on. When we arrived on Monday, we had not only read the assignment but also generated some questions. The entire semester was conducted in this way, and I have to say that it was one of the most inspirational classes I've ever experienced. The professor taught and lectured and led discussions from the questions we asked about the material. Although I don't use this method throughout the semester, some days I do find that answering student questions stimulates more engagement than asking my own.

Serious teachers—by which I mean the teachers we remember, the ones who opened our eyes, maybe even our hearts, to things we might never have known without them—also put much of themselves into their work. This is important. Students come to class wanting to learn not from an automaton but from a living, breathing human being, frailties and all. How much should we disclose of ourselves, our discomforts and vulnerabilities? How much should we keep as our own? I can't answer this for you, but I can say at this stage of my career that many days I have embraced what Saul Bellow said to a class of young writers at Dartmouth: "When I sit at the typewriter, I open my heart. I try to leave nothing covered, suppressed, out of bounds. I give everything I have to that moment." My goal is to do the same in the classroom, making every class period a continual confession of my incurable passion for the subjects I teach.

Of course, the decision to share a personal story is very much related to the style and temperament of the teacher as well as the tone and maturity level of the class. It requires a certain kind of unguardedness, a willingness to run risks, including the risk of making a fool of yourself. During my first year of teaching at the University of Southern California while still a graduate student, I was reasonably confident with the material but not at all confident with myself as a teacher, and so I rarely referenced myself in the lectures and discussions. It took many years before I understood how the telling of illustrative stories from my own experience can help students by showing my human side as well as reminding them of or awakening them to their own vulnerabilities. Sometimes we even discover a hidden truth about ourselves.

What I'm about to tell you, Kelly, I've only recently brought into some of my classes as a way of inviting my students to consider the differences between a story's literal surface structure (as a child would read and understand it) and its deep structure (as an adult would read it).

You know that I grew up in Amherst, Massachusetts, and began taking piano lessons when I was seven. What you don't know is that when I was twelve, each Saturday afternoon I rode my bicycle three miles to the university campus, parked it, and entered the student union to play on the Steinway grand piano that sat in the center room. Usually, the building was empty at this time of day. And so I would imagine that I was about to play a concert at Carnegie Hall. I heard my shoes echo on the tiled hallway floor, then become muffled by the carpet in the sanctuary-like room. I sat at the piano, raised the lid from the keys, and began to play. I played from memory, rudimentally of course, but even then I knew the joy that comes to us when we are absorbed in what we love to do.

One afternoon a sound startled me out of my trance, and I turned around to see a man seated about thirty feet away. I remember that he wore glasses, was balding, and was wearing a maroon sweater and dark blue slacks along with moccasins but no socks. He said nothing—only sat there with his hands clasped in front of him and smiling an enigmatic smile.

The next week he was there again, this time seated closer to the piano. After I had finished playing, he clapped softly. I was flattered. It's nice to know that a stranger appreciates your work—even that of a twelve-year-old. Like most children, I wanted adults to like and respect me.

He asked my name. He told me how much he enjoyed my playing and that he lived only a few blocks from the campus. He asked whether I would like to come to his apartment for some ice cream and strawberries. The invitation was appealing, but something didn't feel right. Was it my mother's repeated warnings about strangers? The cautionary message in a book I'd read? Or was it the instinctive hesitation many children feel when they encounter the unknown? Nevertheless, I agreed to join him.

We sat opposite each other in kitchen chairs. I can see the streaked linoleum floor, the cluttered counters, closed and curtained windows. I remember holding the bowl of vanilla ice cream with the fresh strawberries and cream on top and spooning it into my mouth. I also remember my uneasiness.

All my life I've managed to escape from difficult or unpleasant situations with the spoken word. I wasn't big or strong enough phys-ically to fight my way out, but I could almost always talk faster than most people. I fought with my mouth. And so that afternoon I began to talk about anything—as if I knew instinctively that my chatter would ward off something. What, I didn't know.

Finally, when he offered me more ice cream, I managed to refuse and said: "I'd better go home. My mother will be worried." I left, told no one about the event, and never saw him again. Many months passed before I returned to the campus alone.

As children, we get an idea or see a gesture or participate in an event but we don't really understand it; as we grow, small actions as-sume a larger meaning, subtle nuances assume a clarity that young eyes could not see. Flash forward from that Saturday to forty years later at a different college campus, where I am a faculty member. One day in class, to my surprise (and to my students', too, I am sure), I began to tell the class about this experience. We had been talking about the sometimes deep divide between "seems" and "is," about how one frames the same reality in different ways under dif-ferent circumstances. Suddenly, they understood what the incident might have meant, what could have happened to me, what I had potentially escaped. The deep structure had risen to the surface of their minds, and they understood the value of interpreting events at multiple layers. Then an astonishing thing happened.

As I recounted this story after all those years of silence, the telling itself generated a light-bulb moment, an epiphany. Since my teens, I told my class, I have been aware that I held a vague distrust of people who pay me a compliment. Did they mean it? Did they want some-thing? I never knew why I was so guarded about praise. I just lived with it. Now, as I shared this memory with my class, it suddenly all made sense. This, I thought at the moment, is what learning is all about.

But be careful, Kelly. Relating a personal experience must not be intended to bring attention to us, but to the subject, to shed some light or make possible some insight that goes beyond our own small selves. If stories from our experiences feel to the students to be mere-ly egocentric, then everything that we do in class comes under suspicion. Sincerity and humility are far better teachers than heroics. If when we share some point from our own lives we always come out looking good, if we present ourselves as all-knowing about our subject and our lives, then we won't inspire confidence or questioning or growth in our students. We must not teach as wise, mature, finished people who have learned all the answers, but rather as people who are still asking questions about themselves and about the world, as beings still involved in trying to change, find things out, and do a bit better as humans in community with others.

I can't emphasize this strongly enough: everything we say and do must ultimately bring the students' attention back to the content and away from ourselves. No matter what class we teach, we are not the authorities; the discipline, the long line of scholars who have preceded us, the concepts and ideas and areas of inquiry and fact and thought that define the subject—these are the authorities. We as teachers must become a bridge between—not an impediment to—a corpus of knowledge and those who seek to acquire it.

Students always know somewhere deep inside them whether their teachers are genuine. No gestures, talk, pronouncements can prevail over that deep instinctual knowledge. And so if we expect to be heard and if our aim is to connect with our students, then we must speak with our own voice. This is easier said than done, I know. Most of us, when we start teaching, parrot our own teachers; we teach from outside the material, not inside. Over time, however, good teachers become immersed in their subject. They connect with it in their unique way. Harold Bloom in *The Anxiety of Influence* argues forcefully and convincingly in another context that the primary struggle of the young artist is with the old masters. We must be strong to overcome the anxiety that understandably arises from recognition of the mentor's mastery of the subject. We must acknowledge the influence of our academic precursors, but we must forge our own mastery in our own time. We must be ourselves.

Ultimately, we connect with our students by telling the truth—and the truth is that we are not in class merely to impart information or to help students develop skills. We are there to help our students to see, to wonder, to understand, just as many of our former professors helped us. If I take a photograph of a pastoral setting but fail to focus my lens, the results will be blurry. The scene is recognizable, but my view of it is not. So with us. Our humanity, our inherent limitations, keep us from seeing with clarity. Instead, we see through a glass darkly, says St. Paul. Our vision is obscured, says St. Augustine. We are wanderers in a world of shadows, says Plato, mistaking the outward appearance of people and things for reality. Always, however, something is pressing us to reach out beyond the shadows, to face the reality, to view the truth. With one tiny turn of the lens, our blurred vision can snap into focus—and that is where we, as teachers, come in. Our task is to help our students to develop the eyes to see (and ears to hear) what is new in the old, what is simple in the complex, what is easy in the challenging, what is mundane in the compelling.

"To see is to know," says Astolphe de Custine. My sophomore year taught me that in a special way. I wanted to take a two-semester biology class from a particular professor because he was the best. (That has always been my goal: if you want to learn something, Kelly, seek out the best to learn from; why settle for anything less?) But he taught only pre-med students, and although my minors were science and mathematics, I didn't qualify. The demand for his class was great enough, however, that he agreed to offer an 8 a.m. section three days a week—with lecture on Monday and Wednesday, lab on Friday. I enrolled.

The first week of lab he gave me a slide with something mounted on it and said, "Mr. Salwak, examine the specimen under a microscope and write a report on what you see." Now this was the era when electron microscopes were just being introduced—a wondrous state-of-the-art piece of equipment through which vistas heretofore closed to us were opened. So I devoted the fifty minutes of lab to studying the slide, wrote a paragraph on what I'd seen, and turned it in—feeling quite good about the results. The following Monday, the professor returned my assignment. He had written at the top in red ink: "Looking is not seeing. Try again."

The next Friday, I again slipped the slide under the microscope and examined it. This time I saw more and wrote a full page. I turned it in, again feeling quite good. The following Monday he returned it to me with yet another message written at the top: "You're still not seeing. Try again."

This went on for six weeks until at last I had produced three single-spaced pages of observations. The next Monday he returned the paper to me. At the top were the words: "Good. Now you're seeing!"

He could have told me what was there, he could have given me the vocabulary for what I saw, but then I wouldn't have developed on my own the eyes to see. Unfathomable riches are right in front of us—if only we can see, if only we really learn how to use our eyes. What I didn't know at the time but realized later was that this is exactly the lesson Thoreau was teaching me through the examples he collected during his two years at Walden Pond. It was also similar to an incident described in Nathaniel Southgate Shaler's autobiography, in which the author was asked to examine not a specimen mounted on a slide but a fish. In these examples and many others I have since encountered, the lesson is clear: to think we gain total understanding with one glance, one inspection, one reading is both naïve and foolish. The value of looking at something very closely over a period of time is that we take our eyes off ourselves and begin to appreciate the layers of what is in front of us.

A fundamental principle in teaching is that no two classes are ever the same. Each time we have the privilege of standing before a group of students, we learn a bit more about how to "sell" the material and about how to overcome the fresh challenges that greet us. We also learn more about ourselves. Most of all, the chance to connect with our students and the resulting joy when we succeed is what lures us into the classroom day after day, night after night.

To follow the injunction at the end of E. M. Forster's *Howard's End*, "Only connect . . ."

Warm regards,

CHAPTER 4

A Pastor's Heart

Dear Kelly,

You asked me what it means to have a "pastor's heart" for your students. Well, John Milton in his poem *Lycidas* tells us what it does *not* mean. He writes of self-satisfied shepherds who are in the sheepfold not to care for the sheep but only to satisfy their own self-interests. They haven't bothered to learn their craft. They scarcely know how to hold the tools they are supposed to use. While they eat and drink and attend to their own needs, "The hungry sheep look up, and are not fed." Milton calls these pretenders, "Blind mouths." Jacques Barzun picks up on this theme when he says the archenemy of true teaching is *hokum*: "Words without meaning, verbal filler, artificial apples of knowledge" that leave the learner hungry.

This may surprise you (but not Milton) to hear, but having a pastor's heart for our students is not really a matter of making sure they like us. It's nice if they do, of course, but more important, how much and how freely are we willing to give of ourselves? Do we know the material and are we up-to-date? Can we communicate it clearly and truthfully? Are we reasonable in our expectations of them? Are we fair in our evaluation of their work? Do we listen to what they have to say? Above all, do we treat them as individuals, each unique and brimming with potential?

If you can answer "yes" to these questions, then your students, in turn, will respect and trust you, and reciprocal respect and trust, I am convinced, are the keys to a fruitful educational experience. It begins with our own attitude toward the subjects and the texts we are studying, and extends to the students with whom we are engaged in a common quest for learning. If we fail to demonstrate genuine interest in and enthusiasm for not just the *subjects* of but also the *spirit* of academic inquiry, we are failing our flock. It's disrespectful to our students, and certainly to our colleagues, to arrive at class unprepared, or to complain about or denigrate the profession among students or the general public. It's insulting and intellectually dishonest to water down our material; the surest way to kill students' interest in any subject is to patronize them. Expect the best of yourself and your students, and that's generally what you'll receive. Teach as if your life (and theirs) depends upon it—because it does. Pour all of yourself into the work. Most days you will leave campus emotionally and mentally exhausted because teaching is a giving out—of yourself, of your knowledge and understanding, and of the truth.

At the same time, don't pretend to omniscience. We can teach only what we know. If you can't answer a question, then admit it, and find the answer. I discovered early on that one of the most powerful and liberating tools in my teacher's toolbox was the phrase, "I don't know." Rather than diminishing your stature, this simple admission coupled with, "but I'll look it up," increases it. You aren't expected to know it all.

I remember well my commencement exercises in June 1974 to receive my Ph.D. This rite of passage filled me with joy and the pride of achievement, but I also felt not a few moments of deep anxiety. Now I was in control of the books to read, the essays to write, the discussions to conduct, and the questions to answer. Gone was the reassurance of an exceedingly partitioned life of classes, assignments, and examinations, all of them guided by someone else whose job it was to "know." Now I was on my own, and despite nine years of higher education and three years of teaching experience, I realized how little I knew. If you can admit this to yourself, you can admit it to your students. Pretense rarely becomes a successful learning experience; students see through it, and it collapses quickly.

Respect extends even further—to yourself and your position. Don't take your appointment for granted. Remember where you came from, how hard a climb up the educational ladder it has been for you, and that across the country thousands of nontenured teachers or newly minted Ph.D.'s would be delighted to have your position in the academy. All of us continue to benefit mightily from those who preceded us. Unmerited favor, or grace, has visited us more times than we can count—beginning with the fact that our parents gave us life and sustained it, that we live in a country where we are free to think and study as we wish, that educational opportunities abound, and that were it not for our own teachers, both good and bad, none of us would be privileged to stand where we now stand in the classroom.

As a consequence, I've never forgotten my years as a student. Like you, I remember the all-night study sessions, the anxieties and rewards, the struggles and disappointments as if they occurred yesterday. I also remember the frustrations. One of my graduate professors gave me my only C. On one of my essays he had written, "You seriously underestimate the intellectual integrity of your subject," and on another, "Your conclusions are at best whimsical." Try as I might, I couldn't rise to his expectations. I very well may have deserved the grade, but I suspect he had stereotyped me from the first day of class. A twenty-one-year-old who looked sixteen, I walked in and took my seat among ten peers, all of whom were in their early thirties or older. The professor scanned the room and said to me, "Everybody else looks like your grandparent." It seemed to me that he was already suggesting I didn't measure up. I tried not to let this subtle discrimination discourage me. I worked doubly hard and learned a great deal, but still received that C. Not content with the grade or the experience, I retook the course from another professor and earned an A.

Once as an undergraduate I found myself among three hundred other students in a political science course. Everything about the way the class was taught discouraged me from wanting to learn, including the cavernous lecture hall; the objective, electronically graded tests with two hundred questions; and the remote, inaccessible professor who seemed to teach not because he wanted to but because he had to. I received my only F in four years, and then took the class again from another professor (in a room of thirty students) and received an A.

In neither instance was I making excuses for myself or looking for an easy way out, for I've always worked best when expectations are highest. But on these occasions the expectations the professors communicated were low to nil. I wasn't asking them to make an exception for me, only to evaluate me fairly, as an individual. It seems that, for whatever reasons, these men had lost—or perhaps they never possessed—the respect for their subject, their students, and their profession that nurtures true learning. They'd forgotten what it's like to sit in the student's seat.

Fortunately, these experiences were exceptions. Most of my professors began each semester with much more positive and productive attitudes. They expected all of us to be bright and ambitious. Not all of us were, of course, but they thought and acted as if we were, or could be. As one of them said, "Listen, I assume you've read widely, but if I refer to a work or to an author with whom you're unacquainted, pretend that you are—and then go do the reading." I appreciated that statement, for behind it was an assumption that we were competent, caring partners in a shared academic endeavor.

Along with all that, I learned some lessons about sensitivity that have stayed with me all of my professional life. I learned to see and hear myself through my students' eyes. I also learned that if I didn't respect them and care for the subject I teach, if I sailed through the weeks and months grudgingly loaded with resentments, then I had no place in the classroom—for it ought to be a sacred space in which participants confront the truth free and fearless, hand to hand, face to face.

How do we convey this respect? First, by honoring students' time. Of course, the best way to honor this is to do everything in your power to make the class period stimulating, challenging, and meaningful. Your students have given you their most valuable possession, their *time*. In your allotted span as a professional you must fill it to the peak of your ability and beyond. This means planning, preparing, and being flexible enough to adapt to students' needs. It means really thinking through assignments and ensuring that the hours students will spend on them are hours well invested to achieve specific, attainable objectives.

Honoring students' time also means returning essays and exams promptly, ideally the next class period. To delay two weeks or more is to undermine the very educational purpose for which these assignments are designed. Remember those classes in which an assignment was returned a month later—long after you'd forgotten what you'd written? When I return papers, as often as possible I leave them in the room ten minutes before class so that the students can pick them up when they arrive. Why? Again to save time, and to give them a chance to review my comments and prepare any questions they may have. After we've reviewed the answers in class, I invite them to write their comments or questions and return the papers to me the next day for a response. This not only saves class time but also preserves their privacy, particularly if someone has scored poorly and is reluctant to ask questions before his or her peers.

Honoring their time also means filling out a seating chart, not only to help you to memorize their names but also to save minutes taking roll. I believe taking attendance sends a message to students that says, "I have noticed you, and I care that you are here." After all, their presence in the classroom is a critical component of the learning process. So I keep attendance records; in a mere thirty seconds I can look over the chart and place a checkmark by the name of any missing or late students. To take verbal roll every day means five minutes spent on this mundane chore, which adds up to fifteen minutes a week, which becomes one hour a month or four hours a semester—long enough to read another book.

Finally, honoring students' time means being where they need you to be. If possible, this means unlocking the classroom door early enough so that students can settle in and prepare for the class. (I don't like to arrive to find that thirty students are waiting for me outside a locked classroom door. I prefer to have them seated and settled beforehand so that we can get down to business.) You also need to keep your commitment to class times and office hours. We've all had a professor who steadily missed office hours or was absent from class without advance notice. Sometimes this is unavoidable—illnesses or emergencies or appointments do interrupt. But with the miracle of e-mail we can inform students in advance if we can't make a class so that they don't have to come to campus unnecessarily. Again, this shows respect for them and their busy schedules. (Remember the mixed feelings of relief and annoyance when you traveled all the way to campus to find a "class canceled" notice on the door?)

To some, these might seem to be minor matters, but the tiny details can make a difference in students' attitudes and expectations. How can we require of them the disciplines of punctuality, common sense, and civility if we ourselves don't practice them?

As teachers we also owe it to our students to keep growing. Your classes can advance only as far as you have; students learn as you learn. Upon hearing that I've been teaching for thirty-five years, some might ask, "Haven't you grown tired of teaching the same classes semester after semester, year after year?" With respect, only a non-teacher could ask that question. Why would I grow tired of doing what I've dreamed of since I was fourteen? No two semesters are ever the same. New students require new strategies. Personal growth invites new lectures and approaches. From good classes we often learn as much as we hope the students learn from us. Heraclitus has it right when he says, "You cannot step into the same river [of thought] twice."

According to Henry James, the novelist is one "upon whom nothing is lost." This strikes me as a welcome definition of a teacher, whose personal experiences and professional training are woven inextricably into what he or she brings to the classroom. As you have already discovered, Kelly, this is a twenty-four-hour-a-day, twelve-months-a-year commitment. Everything we take in is grist for the mill. An overheard conversation might become a suitable illustrative anecdote. A new book might add an unexpected angle to a lecture or discussion. A personal experience might communicate in a fresh, contemporary way a truth you have discovered from your readings. Nothing that happens to a teacher need ever be wasted.

Sometimes an accident turns out to be an advantage. One day at the end of an exam, I watched a student drop her notes into the trash can on her way out. I discretely retrieved the pages, stapled them together, and returned them to her the next day with an attached message: "You'll need these for the final exam." She was surprised, and chagrined, I'm sure, to have been found out. Without calling attention to her, I was able to use this as an opportunity to speak to the class about the importance of valuing their notes, not only for our class but for years ahead. "You'll never regret it," I said. Then I added: "On the top shelf of a ceiling-high bookcase in my office I keep thirty-one notebooks from my years as a high school and university student. Tucked into three file drawers is another five year's worth of graduate school papers. These collections are like time capsules, charged with sentiment: I would no more toss them away than my mother would discard her two sons' baby clothes." Both the student's action and my own experiences became an important object lesson in the techniques and value of learning. Neither was "lost."

Of course, to keep growing we must also keep reading—an activity so necessary to the nourishment and stimulation of the mind and spirit that it's beyond my imagining how people can get through their professional lives without it (although you know some who do). Steep yourself in the best not only in your discipline but across subjects, genres, and periods. Read for information, read for stimulation, read for fun. The transformative effect of books is shown by David McCullough so magnificently in his biography of the second American president, John Adams. The son of an illiterate farmer, Adams discovered books at Harvard, started reading—and never stopped. "His zeal for books would be his last passion to desert him," said Abigail of her husband when he was eighty. As president he established the Library of Congress.

We are what we read. If we want to know the truth of other people, then read what they have read. When I was thirteen I learned that one of my maternal grandmother's favorite novels was A. J. Cronin's *Keys of the Kingdom*. Next day I pulled her copy from the bookshelf and began to read it—because I wanted to know her better. (I could never have guessed that twenty-five years later I would be led to write a biography of the author.) This principle applies to the classroom. You might like to begin each semester with a questionnaire on which you ask your students to list by title (and author if they can remember) up to ten books that have significantly affected their thinking; then ask them to choose one, and explain why. Doing this will help you to put together a personal reading list for the new semester. Most important, it communicates to them that the book is not dying, that reading is not an elitist and antiquated passion, and that you are genuinely interested in knowing each student as an individual.

It's also vital to stay fresh in your field and on top of the research because one of your obligations is to advise students on what they should read. An English major, for instance, might find early on that there are more than six thousand published books on Shakespeare's life and work. She couldn't possibly read all of them, nor would she want to, but out of that mountain she will want to read a couple dozen volumes of secondary materials if she is to be well grounded in Renaissance literature. It's your responsibility, Kelly, to know the contours of the research and to make recommendations, just as many of your own professors did for you. Then it's up to the students to buckle down and do the work.

Our growth as professionals also depends on the community of teachers. Along with committee obligations, social gatherings, and workshops, one of the most useful activities on my campus has been a "What Professors Read" conference. Many of the students and faculty members gather for an afternoon to hear seven of us talk about a favorite book, followed by an hour-long question-and-answer session.

You can bring the "What Professors Read" concept into your class by letting the students know of your current reading list. Make recommendations, and invite them to offer their own reading suggestions. In my Advanced Rhetoric class, for example, the second essay assignment asks students to evaluate a book of their choice. My promise is that if I haven't read the book, I will do so. The positive effects this announcement has on their self-esteem and the seriousness with which they approach their own work are well worth the effort it takes to read some additional books—and the bonus for me is discovering new works I hadn't encountered before.

As you can see, I believe that the teacher-student relationship is an emotional as well as an intellectual one, often complex and unstable. Sometimes no matter how respectful and earnest we are, however, some students will remain unmovable. To them, perhaps, education is a long, endless row of obligations to be fulfilled, and nothing more. Or they arrive with a back load of years spent listening to lectures, reading books, and writing papers with a constantly increasing resentment. Or they have become stymied by fear of rejection or insecurity about their own abilities. Or worse.

The first day of my Literature of the Bible class, in walked a middle-aged woman, wearing a Coors beer can hat impaled with fishhooks. I soon learned that before every class, she went fishing for a couple of hours. At my request, she left her tackle box and rod outside.

She sat in the back row, corner seat, but with her arms crossed the entire class period; she never once lifted her pen to take notes. One day I asked her why not. She said, without irony: "Well, I already know everything there is to know about the subject. I'm just here to make sure you stay on the mark."

Some teachers might have taken offense at this remark, but I was curious to see where this would lead. If she didn't disrupt the class then she was welcome to stay there. So I said, amiably but emphatically, "Fine, and if I ever do slip off the mark, be sure to let me know." I continued to lecture and ask questions of the class with renewed vigor as she sat scowling, arms crossed.

Six weeks later she came to my office. "I've decided to drop the class," she said. "It really is beneath me."

"You know," I said, "I think you're absolutely right." I signed her pink drop slip without delay and never saw her again.

Perhaps given different circumstances or another teacher, this woman's attitude would change. I can't be sure, but I couldn't make her the center of my attention—tempting as it was. Resentment, anger, or dominance has no place in the portfolio of a professor's emotions. Our students expect more of us. Through our reading and study, we've spent too many years in the company of great minds to be distracted or intimidated by the arrogance of one student. We must never sacrifice the many for the sake of the one.

Sometimes the ideals of the classroom are challenged or even denigrated by those outside it. Once I related to a nonacademic friend an account of a class discussion. I had been exploring the theme of marriage in fairy tales with my students, and one asked, "If the wife dies, should the widower remarry?"

"I can't answer that," I said. "I believe that if there are children, it would depend on what's best for them." As I explained, when we first marry, we do so for ourselves. If we remarry, and if there are children still living at home, then our needs must be secondary to theirs.

The consequences of ignoring this principle are dramatized in many classic fairy tales—such as "Cinderella" or "Hansel and Grethel"—in which the father, after the death of his loving, warmhearted wife, remarries a haughty, overbearing woman. (Why he does so is left to the reader's imagination.) The story then explores the unpleasant consequences upon the lives of the children as the stepmother assumes control of the family and the father recedes into the background, compliant and passive. The message here is not that the stepmother is bad, but that the father chose the wrong woman. Had he married another kind of woman, the children may have greatly benefited.

"You spend class time discussing *that*?" my friend asked. This is the same friend who, when I told him that I start to re-prepare my classes six months in advance, said, "For an *English* class?"

"Yes," I said, "we discuss such things because the literature evokes them, and because they matter."

Hinted at in my friend's question is an age-old prejudice. Always and everywhere there will be those who sneer at what we do in (or out of) the classroom. Like it or not, some people think academicians to be underworked and overpaid, unrealistic and isolated, doing very little in general and in particular only what they like. Of course it would be dishonest to say that this is never true. Every profession, including teaching, attracts a certain number of individuals who do not belong there. Milton calls what they do the "sin of non-teaching." But they are in the minority; although nonacademics might not comprehend the intensity of what we do and the dedication it requires of us, its value is apparent in every "Aha!" moment that lights up a student's face.

As much as you enjoy connecting with your students, it's essential to find some quiet time, just for yourself, and to counsel students to do the same. Every hour in class is the culmination of many more hours out of class devoted to quiet reflection, study, preparation, and re-preparation. We must respect and cultivate that creative, isolated time. A teacher must be often alone, and it is just as well to discover our tolerance for that early on—the earlier, the better.

Each of us needs a room of our own where we can just be, unencumbered, so that we may "become acquainted" (to use Emerson's phrase) with our thoughts. On the University of Southern California campus there used to sit an easy-to-miss, gray-stone chapel that provided a place for private prayer and meditation. I had to stoop like a child to enter a room just large enough to hold five or six people. Everything about its interior—the wooden beams that ribbed the ceiling, the dark green carpeting, the gingerbread-colored pew benches—was designed to promote an atmosphere of tranquil happiness.

During my graduate years I went there every Friday, sometimes alone, sometimes with two or three members of my weekly study group. We came with our needs—and we talked, we prayed, we listened. Upon emerging two or three hours later, I felt renewed and strengthened, as if I had just returned from a mountain retreat. I seek those opportunities for withdrawal whenever and wherever I can find them.

Teaching is one of the few professions I know of that protects the right and need of its members to step back from the arena and reflect—and therein to grow. Our teaching schedules allow for that, and so does an opportunity awarded to a few applicants every year. I'm referring to the sabbatical—from the same root as the Hebrew *Shabbath* and the more modern *Sabbath*, meaning, "to rest." In their wisdom the Hebrews knew the importance of emulating God's model of resting after the work of creation was finished. The Sabbath allows participants to pause, to put away the distractions of life, to turn from exterior concerns and focus on the inner issues. It is a day of physical rest and spiritual revitalization. It is an essential time when we take in rather than give out, when we stop to realize what we have accomplished, what we have made, and where we should go from there. Just so with the teaching sabbatical.

Oftentimes the sabbatical marks a turning point in the life of the recipient. It means carrying on advanced study in any field under the freest possible conditions. It means following our professional inclinations wherever they may lead. It means becoming a student again in the classroom of the world. It means having time to read more slowly and widely and deeply, to return to books that speak to us with a special intimacy. It means finding time for rejuvenation, for redefinition, for relaxation. After all, as the Greeks well understood, the best use for leisure is to study.

More than earning credits or degrees or awards or grades, more than acquiring information, education disciplines and strengthens the mind and teaches students how to think and ask questions and solve problems. It also confers upon them the self-confidence necessary for self-propelling, independent study in the years ahead. Education in the humanities, for example, has to do with books and painting and music and dance and folklore and history and mythology and so much more, all of it important and all of it connected. Deepen your students' appreciation and understanding of one or more of the fine arts, and they'll be better engineers or doctors. Expand their knowledge and application of mathematics and the sciences, and they'll be better public servants. Provide them with the concepts of psychology or anthropology, and they'll be better actors, geneticists, or entrepreneurs. College is where a habit of mind is formed that lasts through life. The secret to this, I am convinced, goes beyond how much we know to how we relate to the students we are privileged to serve.

So, Kelly: what does it mean to have a pastor's heart for your students? It means displaying humility, gratitude, and esteem for them. It means being prepared, careful, courageous, contemplative, and provoking. It means growing, every day, with the skills you have been given.

Service is the lifeblood that flows through the teacher's heart—a subject on which I have more to say, but I'll reserve that for another letter.

Warm regards,

CHAPTER 5

Lecturing

Dear Kelly,

I'm sure that you can relate to the story about the lecturer who, having one week remaining in the term, meets a colleague on his way to class and says, "So far I've covered half the course. I'm giving them the second half today." And no doubt as a student yourself, on occasion you agreed with the sentiment of Immanuel Kant, who once defined the lecture as "a process by which the notes of the professor become the notes of the student without passing through the head of either."

At times you may even have agreed with those who claim that the lecture is outmoded or oppressive, an archaic academic custom rendered ineffectual by television, computers, and cheap and easy access to printed works. Even if reports of the lecture's demise are premature, the unfortunate reality is that too many teachers enter into this instructional form too lightly, pay too little attention to what good lectures might accomplish, and as a result deliver a product that is too far gone to be resuscitated.

Nevertheless, like many of my colleagues, I believe that if composed and delivered with care, a lecture can be one of the liveliest and most effective strategies for engaging the minds of students at any level of the curriculum—and for promoting understanding, sharing knowledge, and imparting a sense of what it means to be a part of the academy. I have also learned that lecturing is an art not to be taken lightly or for granted.

Thinking back to the professors I had who taught almost exclusively by lecturing, I can single out perhaps two dozen who were highly effective because they caught and held our attention, provided emphasis and direction, led up to a key moment, and then struck home. I remember these professors as being keenly aware of and responsive to their students, well organized, able to justify the importance of the material, and often highly entertaining. Their endless curiosity and command of the material was unquestioned; their presentations were precise and compact; and yet they invited us to interrupt their lectures at any time for questions, further discussion, even challenges, to which they respectfully responded without making us feel like complete fools for raising them.

Usually their lectures sounded spontaneous and fresh, although I am sure that they had worked and reworked the material over many semesters, if not years. Their voice quality and articulation were effective, even pleasing, without such maddening verbal afflictions as repeated *uhs* and *ers* and *you-knows*; and rarely did we have to strain to hear what they were saying or guess at stress and emphasis or organization of sentences. Most of all, they were never predictable.

If it's true that the mark of a great professor lies not only in what is taught or how, but also in what happens in the mind of a receptive student, then these particular professors were truly great. And if I have had any success as a lecturer in the classroom, it is in large part due to the examples set by many of these men and women to whom, as an aspiring teacher myself, I listened as much for technique as for content. Now that I stand before my own students, lectures are a major class component, balanced often with discussion and questions, sometimes with recitation, occasionally by demonstration.

In planning lectures, I like to start at the end and work backwards. Where do I want to lead the students? What do I hope they will carry with them from the classroom? These are among the questions I ask myself as I try to see the big picture for the entire semester during my preparation. Without clarity and a sense of purpose, one aims at nothing—and usually hits it. I need a clearly defined goal that I can target.

After I have identified the goals and completed most of the background reading, research, and thinking on the subject, I'm ready to compose the lecture itself. The word *invent* comes from the Latin word *invenire*, which means "to make" or "to create"; but it also means "to find." In some special way, I believe we find within ourselves what is already there. "Making things plain to uninstructed people," says T. H. Huxley, can be "one of the very best means of clearing up the obscure corners in one's own mind." Surely one of the most exciting elements of teaching is that we get to communicate and test not only other scholars' knowledge but also our own discoveries in the very process of their being made—or revised.

To help myself do so, I try to divide the term into blocks of materials, each block corresponding to one week and defining its own piece in the whole mosaic I hope to create. I concentrate on facts first, and then try to find concrete illustrations to develop, and I give to each week of material a beginning, a middle, and an end. All this I reduce to a one- or two-page topic outline from which I will lecture and lead the discussion spontaneously.

Spontaneity is the key here. The most meaningful classes for me as a student were not those in which I was force-fed a prescribed diet of dry facts and unappetizing, bland concepts. What drove me every day (and still does) was the thrill of discovery as we explored the subject together—with honesty and lucidity and courage. In other words, we were transformed from hearers to participants in our own and others' learning process.

For this reason, I believe that lectures must be punctuated with lots of hard questions—mine and those of the students. I expect everyone to come to class having reviewed their notes from the previous meetings. My opening question—"What don't you understand?"— invites them to ask anything about what we've covered so far. It's a way of looking back so that we can then move ahead. There's little point in presenting new concepts if they haven't grasped the old. I'm not necessarily interested in how much material students can memorize or how many details they can churn out on an examination. Almost anyone with a modest amount of effort can achieve that. I *am* interested in how much they understand and how much they broaden and deepen their *ability* to understand, and both require hard thinking on their part, and focus and patience on mine.

Sometimes, I will pose as knowing nothing and invite my students to teach me, meanwhile pushing them with probing questions. This strategy serves to bring out all sides of an argument. Or I will devote an entire class period to questions and answers, especially as a review strategy before an exam. If I'm not satisfied with their first answer to a question, then I might have to ask "why" several times before the students discover what they really think and know, and I encourage them to expect the same from me. Remember: the Latin root for *to educate* is related to *educere*—which means "to lead forth." Our role is to help students find answers within themselves and then lead them forward.

Midway in the semester, I take a cue from James Phelan's *Beyond the Tenure Track* and distribute a form that asks students to complete two sentences: "(1) For these final eight weeks, I hope that this course/teacher will continue to . . . ; and (2) Before this semester is over, I hope that this course/teacher will begin to . . ." If a shift in approach is needed, this evaluation will signal it for you. When a class isn't going well, always assume the problem is with you, not with your students.

With the ending and middle of a lecture clearly in mind, I can work on the beginning—a crucial component because, if done well, it helps to establish the focus for the day, sets a tone of high expectations, prepares the way for what is to come, and is the "hook" for catching the listeners' attention and linking the previous class periods to the present one. Over the years I have accumulated a small file of strategies for beginning a class. The following are among my favorites.

Sometimes I open with a direct question about the assigned reading or an anecdote or a lesson from history. Occasionally I like to begin by pointing out the relevance of the text, that it has something to say, and I challenge the students to discover it. Or I might simply state the central point of the day, then go on. Opening with a brief show-and-tell exercise of relevant books works well, as does covering a current (and pertinent) news item that may be on their minds and provides a link to my context.

One day I walked into the room and without saying a word I wrote the following words on the board: vulgar, inelegant, ungrammatical, coarse, irreverent, vicious. Then I said, "What do these words describe? (1) Moral disapproval of *The Adventures of Huck-*

leberry Finn as expressed by some readers; (2) your own reactions to the text; or (3) your professor." After their hoped-for laughter, I moved on to discuss the insidious threats of censorship in the news at the time and why this much-loved classic has unsettled some readers ever since it was published in 1885.

Also effective at times is to pull a personal story from my life. One semester, for example, I opened my class on Classics of Children's Literature with these words: "I have a son named Ryan. In his few years he has traveled to India, to Africa, to much of Europe; he has visited most of America's fifty states; he has seen the Mayan ruins, the Egyptian pyramids, and the Alps. He has descended twenty thousand leagues under the sea, climbed to the top of Mount Everest, and ridden into orbit aboard a spaceship. His footsteps are in the dust of Mars, Mercury, and the moon. He has stared into the eyes of a Tyrannosaurus Rex."

Halfway through this, my students realized that I was speaking of the power of the imagination—leading to a lecture-discussion on the effects of the printed word upon the creative life of a child.

At other times I find it appropriate to retell a story the students have read out of class, but I purposefully make mistakes. During a lecture on the book of Genesis, for example, I began with these words: "And God said to Abraham, 'Take your son, your only son Isaac, whom you love, and go to the land of Moriah, and offer him there as a burnt offering on one of the mountains that I shall show you.' But Abraham, perceiving immediately what God was asking of him, turned with a heavy heart and said, 'My God, not Isaac, my son, my only son whom I love. Take Ishmael, son of Hagar, or someone else, but surely you will not require me to slay my only son whom thou promised to me so many years before!'"

In the biblical account, as you know, Abraham obeys God's command without hesitation or complaint. My incorrect version is a lighthearted way of ensuring that the students have read the assignment carefully—and from there we may look at what the text *does* say and does *not* say, how it says it, and why. My first target in every class I teach is not what students *think* the text says, not what they *hope* it says, not even necessarily what they've *been told* it says—but rather what it *does* say. Only after we have agreed on its literal meaning can we then consider the suggestive power of the words in all their eloquence. With other literature, however, I don't necessarily insist upon a particular interpretation. I *suggest* one (or two or three) while at the same time pointing out that the classics we study have touched readers generation after generation, often in ways that transcend the intentions of the originating author. I stress that the *process* of interpretation is probably more crucial than the interpretation itself. I have sat through one too many Socratic explorations, each arriving at some wonderfully transcendental discovery, only to leave it there and never step back to ask, "Now what just happened there?" "How did we do that?"

As important as the opening of a lecture is, no less important is the closing. Students want to be challenged, and so we must aim to leave them wanting more. Here I take a lesson from Hemingway, who ended each day of writing by stopping on an incomplete note, either leaving a scene purposefully unfinished or getting on paper the opening of the next scene. This generated a suspenseful finish, guaranteed that the next day would get off to a possibly easy start, and conveyed some sense of continuity.

You can do the same in class, Kelly. The simplest way to achieve this is to give students a preview of "coming attractions," thereby leaving them with something to think about. Or conclude with a question toward which the lecture has been building, and then say that you'll answer it next time.

After assigning Yeats's "The Second Coming," for example, I said: "Let's see how well you know me. At our next meeting be prepared to identify the two memorable lines that have haunted me since tenth grade when I first heard the poem read aloud." (I also explained that this was at the time of the Cuban missile crisis.)

The next class, I began with that question, and indeed many of them had guessed correctly: "And what rough beast, its hour come round at last, / Slouches towards Bethlehem to be born?" Then we discussed why this poem, like all great poems, always speaks to our condition no matter the time, and why after the September 11th terrorist attacks on the United States, "The Second Coming" and

W. H. Auden's "September 1, 1939" were among the most frequently quoted poems over the Internet.

Of course, the researching and writing of lectures is not as organized, as straightforward, or as predictable as suggested here. Each semester and each class are different, and good lecturers many times need to follow their instincts. One presentation cannot fit all hearers in all conditions and all situations. Between semesters (if not between classes) I find myself reshaping and refocusing the material to fit a particular class. Each group of students has its own pace and mood; some students are more adept at making the material relevant to their own lives, a process that, in an ideal world, they would perform independently but in the real world may require guidance. Some groups have their own synergy; others need more support. An experienced teacher has learned to evaluate those needs and adjust the material and other learning activities appropriately. Much of your success as a lecturer will derive from the close connection you establish between your students and yourself. That connection allows you to assess where your students are in relation to your goals and will help you guide them toward where they need to be.

As a speaker, therefore, never forget the importance of knowing your audience. All great teachers who taught by the spoken word—Moses, Pythagoras, the Buddha, Socrates, Jesus, for example—adapted and responded to the needs of their listeners before guiding them to where they yearned to be. On the first day, Kelly, you might ask for students' written answers to three questions: "(1) What do you perceive to be the purpose of this course? (2) What is the value and validity of the subject? (3) What confuses you about it?" (After a few years of this, you'll be able to predict most of their answers.) Then on the back side ask them to list at least five questions about the subject that they would like to have answered during the semester. The results will help you to clarify for them (if necessary) the course objectives and to persuade those who need to be persuaded that what they will be studying does indeed matter. Many weeks later as part of the final exam, return their questionnaires and ask them how they would now answer these questions—thereby affirming what they've learned and why they've learned it.

I also make conscious attempts to integrate the latest findings of research into my lectures; and sometimes I give the students the benefit of the doubt by using the words, "As you know," with an aim toward drawing them into the partnership of learning as fellow scholars and thinkers rather than as passive vessels. Of course, in most instances the students do *not* know what I am about to say. But that is all part of my philosophy of coming to class with high expectations, for I have learned that diminished expectations yield diminished results. Every day, try to leave your students with this thought: "I can't believe how much we covered!"

Remember, too, that your calling as a teacher is not to reshape yourself to fit the surrounding culture but to become a significant force in *shaping* that culture. Please don't misapply the word *like* (as in, "I'm, like, going to tell you about the exam"), or use the word *goes* when you mean *says*, or raise your voice at the end of a sentence that is not a question, or conclude a statement with the word *whatever*. When one of my students said, "Well, Jesus was crucified, or whatever," I stopped everything, and for the rest of the period we discussed how and why the Romans used this brutal means of execution, which they had learned from the Carthaginians. Like you, I lament the decline of the English language in so many sectors. Everywhere, it seems, public speakers care less and less about which words they use. Communication establishes a bond, a tie to another human being; undermining communication ultimately undermines humanity. So as communicators, we must do our best to convey our message through both words and example. If it's worth saying, it's worth saying well.

Our respect for the students we serve is married to our respect for the language we use. Never underestimate the power of the spoken word. Lives have been changed with a simple *yes* or *no* or *I do*. A few words have begun and concluded wars, broken or cemented friendships, begun or ended marriages. Listen to your vocabulary, syntax, phraseology, and patterns of speech. Don't use a three- or four-syllable word when a shorter one will do. Don't muddle your way through sentences, frequently failing to finish them. Don't smack your lips. Don't chew gum. Be aware of how you sound. Tone (your attitude toward the students and the material) is everything. If necessary, take another speech class and learn more about breath control, projection, and pitch. Repeated hesitations, interruptions, or false starts only distract listeners from the experience of deep thinking. Our purpose is not to engage in small talk or jargon (we do plenty of that outside the classroom), nor is it in most instances our job to be politically correct (what Martin Amis calls "a series of polite fictions"). Our purpose is to impart understanding and to model modes of expression that enrich rather than dilute language.

Sometimes, however, our eccentricities can help to establish a favorable rhythm to the classroom proceedings. In the years before the laws against indoor smoking, I had an American literature professor who held a lighted pipe throughout the three-hour class. He would speak for several minutes, then stop to take a draw, exhale, and continue with what he had been saying. At least once each class period he paused, walked to the open window, tapped the pipe against the outside wall, and then removed from his inner coat pocket a tobacco pouch. I'd watch intently as he refilled the pipe with fresh tobacco, returned the pouch to his pocket, lit the tobacco, took several long draws, and then continued speaking. (One day, curious, I walked outside the classroom and found beneath his window a seven-inch mound of dried, burnt tobacco. He'd been performing this ritual for many years.) At the time I thought this odd, but later I realized his performance was a brilliant strategy for holding our attention while giving us time to catch up with our notes and think over what he had said. More than likely the pause gave him time to collect his thoughts, too.

You should also remember, I think, that less is more. Early in my career a dean advised me to cut everything in half for one of my classes. "Imposing an excessive workload on your students," he said, "is a symptom of inexperience." He was correct. From thirty assigned short stories, I cut to fifteen; from six required essays, I cut to three; and from twelve quizzes, I cut to six. Now I would rather keep my undergraduate students interested in and involved with a close study of twenty texts spread over the semester than force their minds to drift by rushing through thirty or forty texts; and I would rather have them take their time and develop four essays than crank out eight or more just for the sake of completing the assignments. Quality rather than quantity encourages deeper, clearer thinking, greater intellectual development, and a stronger grasp of material and skills.

Although in practice I wouldn't recommend this, in theory one could take most any classic novel or poem or play and teach from that one text just about everything a student might be expected to learn of a particular literary period. As you know from your own graduate study, individual works can seem to be almost infinitely rich and layered. I remember your telling me that you learned an enormous amount about Renaissance literature from a fourteen-week seminar on Milton's *Paradise Lost*, and that your understanding of twentieth-century British literature exploded after a seminar devoted to James Joyce's *Dubliners*, *Portrait of the Artist as a Young Man*, and *Ulysses*. The more we look at a specific work, the more we see. Taking time for that kind of careful examination of fewer works enhances learning and helps student develop critical thinking skills that they can apply as they extend their reading repertoire throughout their lives.

Finally, you asked me to comment on the value of technology in the classroom. I'm reminded of a professor who would leave behind a taped lecture whenever he was absent. Students arrived, pushed the "on" button, and listened while taking notes for the next hour. After several of these episodes, the students had had quite enough. One day he returned to find that no students were waiting for him—only thirty tape recorders.

In brief, if I'm teaching serious literature, art, or philosophy, I prefer a blackboard, the text, my students—and nothing more. In some instances I have used visual aids (overheads, slides, movies, VHS, or media displays) if they enhance (and do not distract from) the learning experience. More often I have distributed printouts of illustrations or photographs so that the students could write on them and study them more closely than they could if viewed on a screen.

Although I can well understand its allure, I rarely use PowerPoint because it strikes me as a bit canned and artificial—like a ghostwritten book or the laugh track of a sitcom. It lacks spontaneity and verve and life. I prefer to write my thoughts on the board as I'm lecturing. If I rely on technology to do that for me, then I don't necessarily have to think through each sentence I speak to its conclusion. There's less opportunity for fresh ideas to pop up and less freedom to shape the message to fit my students' needs. I want the students to feel we are discovering new ideas as we move along with the material. Also, why does a student have to be in the classroom at all if the teacher relies on a PowerPoint presentation? He or she might just as well be given a printout to read at home.

If you do use media, first weigh the philosophical and practical implications. My suspicion is that many times we turn to technology because it makes teaching easier—*for us*. This seems to me a risky reason to proceed. We should change or adapt *only* if by doing so we better serve the students.

If you do use the media, don't waste class time setting up the equipment or solving problems or acquainting yourself with its operation. Take care of all that beforehand.

And if you do use media, never let it vitiate the *human* connection between yourself and your students. "A worthwhile university or college," says George Steiner, "is quite simply one in which the student is brought into personal contact with, is made vulnerable to, the aura and threat of the first-class." Exactly.

Well, this is quite enough for one day. I'll bring this letter to a close by relating a story. Isaac Stern describes how it felt to experience the teaching of the great cellist Pablo Casals: "Imagine yourself suddenly coming upon a wall, not knowing that beyond it lay an exquisite garden. What Casals did was open a door into the garden; you entered and suddenly found yourself amid colors and scents you never dreamed existed. He revealed what might be accomplished once you were inside the garden. But how many of the colors and scents you could make your own, giving greater power to your musical imagination—that was your responsibility."

I have never heard or read a more fitting description of the role that a professor-as-lecturer can play in the lives of students. In any subject, the teacher shows to students the possibilities the new learning can engender. Then those students must discover for themselves what to do with what they have been shown.

As a teacher, Kelly, I believe you can lead your charges to that door and open it if you create and deliver lectures that guide, stimulate, and inspire mature thinking and intelligent inquiry.

Warm regards,

CHAPTER 6

Choices

Dear Kelly,

On last semester's final exam, as I do every semester, I asked my students to reflect on their work and discuss the effect of our readings, discussions, and other assignments. Among the students' comments were the following:

> I feel I cheated myself from getting all the benefits I could have if I had involved myself more in the readings. I wish I hadn't been so half-hearted.

> I didn't read regularly. I crammed a lot. I know that if I had read every day, I wouldn't have been so lost during the lectures.

> I think I missed a golden opportunity to learn and grow. I let personal matters get in the way of what really counts: my studies.

Why do some students get bogged down? Why do some of them fail to live up to their potential? The answer, I believe, is that they lack a vision for what it means to be an educated person and how the process of learning connects rather than fragments their lives. They don't know why they are studying the material in any given curriculum or where it will take them. They don't know what to expect from a college class or what to look for in a particular discipline. They read text as it appears on its face and have no comprehension of why it says what it says or what it is driving at or why. They have very little motivation to probe into a subject and discover its marvelous secrets. They haven't appropriated what they've learned, having neither engaged nor acted upon it.

Kelly, I'm convinced that most of our students will do about as well in their classes as they *choose* to do, and I believe that it is our responsibility as teachers to give them reasons to care about the material and to choose to do well.

Here, then, are six suggestions that I distribute as a handout to my students on the first day of each semester—to be read and discussed in class. My intention is not to insult their intelligence. Most of them have heard these over and over during their education, but sometimes it's useful to return to the basics. Nor is there anything necessarily original in what follows. These suggestions come from observations, experience, and good advice that I have received during my own years as a student along with my time in the classroom as a teacher. Now that you've embarked on this voyage, perhaps you'll find in them something to motivate your own students to delve more deeply into the transformative examination of the ideas at the heart of a true education.

1. *Attend classes, arrive on time.* Obvious propositions, and yet you might be surprised to learn how many students assume a rather lazy attitude about attendance. In all of my education, I only missed class because of illness, and I was rarely late. I showed up because I had wise parents and counselors who taught me that once I had made a commitment to a course, I must keep it. Missing classes (or arriving late) for reasons other than illness or an emergency invalidates the inherent worth of participating directly in the learning process, of sharing questions and ideas, of observing how minds can inspire each other to grow and strengthen. Electing to withdraw from that intellectual adventure undermines the very nature of the education. As every one of my students understands clearly from the first day of the semester, attendance is not only an obligation but a privilege.

I often wonder what would have happened if I had not heard Mrs. Lewis, my eighth-grade English teacher, speak six words that would change my life. I can see her now, with her smooth white-gold hair, spectacled face, and brilliant sky-blue eyes shining with intelligence and wit. Her class was pure pleasure because she challenged us to set aside our youthful distractions and focus on what mattered. It simply never occurred to her that we were incapable of reading Shakespeare or enjoying the great English poets and major novelists. Sometimes the pressure-cooker ambience of the room was so intense I expected the windows to shatter at any moment. I remember thinking: This is the way *all* classes ought to be conducted.

It was late in May, toward the end of the semester, when she said to our class, "To one of you I am giving an 'A' for the semester. You have earned a 'B+', but I'm giving you an 'A' because [and here are the six words] I think you have the potential." In retrospect, I'm certain that she was speaking to several students, but at the time I believed she was speaking only to me, and that made all the difference.

Those few words, simple yet laden with meaning for that impressionable schoolboy, helped solidify the commitment that carried me through high school, university, and graduate school. Sure, sometimes my dedication flagged, and it would have been easy to skip a class and do something else. But whenever I felt reluctant about completing an assignment, confused about something said in class, fearful about taking an examination, or doubtful of my abilities, like magic there arose within me the words of Mrs. Lewis: *I think you have the potential.* I knew that to find and tap into that potential, I needed to be a present, active participant in the learning community.

As with absences, most excuses for late arrival are unacceptable. Those students who have to drive thirty or more minutes to campus are always on time. It's the ones who merely have to cross the street from home, or walk a block or two, whom I worry about. (If on-time arrival is hard for your students, then perhaps they can do what I've done for years—advance the hands of their clocks by fifteen minutes. This may annoy their friends and family, but they'll be surprised by the effectiveness of such a simple trick. On many occasions I've rushed to a meeting only to realize I have an extra fifteen minutes.) Late arrival distracts the class, breaks peers' focus and concentration on the text, and in general shows a lack of respect for both the professor and the other students. Late arrival also ensures that the students miss key ideas always given during the first five minutes of the class. (They can't learn what they don't hear.) And late arrival breaks the commitment that each student makes when he or she enrolls. We're always on time for what is important to us; encourage your students to make class time important.

2. *Complete all reading assignments before coming to class.* Again, this may strike you as an obvious proposition, but by now you've no doubt discovered that unless they have a solid reason for doing so, some of your students will try to avoid reading at all.

To help them get the most from their class assignments, therefore, advise them that as they read, they should make notes about questions they have, insights they've gained, and areas they'd like to explore further. Encourage them to underline or highlight passages in their reading and to "talk" to their books by scribbling marginal notes. Leave their mark. "A book is like a pair of shoes," says Lynne Sharon Schwartz. "It can't become their favorite until they break it in." I tell my students to get in there and make it their own. If something is said that they don't like or can't believe, argue with the author. Outlining the reading in a notebook also helps; since good lectures and discussions build upon the readings, students must have that foundation already. Rarely do I repeat in class what students have read out of class—unless they ask for clarification or expansion. If they don't read with care and thought and "digest" the material to the best of their ability, then they will benefit very little from what we cover in class. The books we read provide no sanctuary for the superficial reader.

I would also suggest that you warn your students about the trap of neglecting their reading because they dislike an assigned book. They're not being asked to like it but to surrender to it on the author's terms. A mature and accurate judgment about a book comes only after understanding it. Three things matter: Is the book of value, is it challenging, and will it do them any good? Sometimes students seem to resent having good books pressed on them. I respond by asking: "Does it really matter if the reading seems to be beyond your capacity? Does it really matter if you fail to understand all of what you are reading? While developing a taste for good words, you are also developing a taste for thoughts and ideas expressed by minds more learned than your own." The enormous nuances of the English language, the richness of our vocabulary—all this should fill a student with gratitude, not resentment. In tenth grade my teacher assigned us to read Melville's *Moby-Dick*. As I sat there, astonished, with the 540-page novel in my hands, I thought: "My teacher actually trusts me with this. He actually thinks I can read it and understand it." I read avidly and tried hard not to disappoint him.

3. *Consciously engage the material.* Some studies have shown that the attention span of the average American adult is about eleven minutes. Although this may be true, we don't have to accept such failure to focus from our students. Listening is a choice. In most instances we choose to listen to what interests us. So push your students to decide, today, to be interested in the subject, and foster their interest by modeling your own. As one of my professors liked to say: "Lack of interest is not an acceptable excuse for missing class. How can you say you're uninterested in a subject you know so little about?" Almost any subject or person has some inherently interesting quality if we just look for it, and the pull of the material often grows stronger the more we learn about it.

When a task is both interesting and challenging, most of us are willing to work hard to accomplish it. Little encouragement is necessary because achievement is inherently rewarding. But when we are given a task that seems irrelevant or specious, enthusiasm for it is difficult or even impossible to muster. A task we deem unworthy of our efforts or consideration will receive neither. How often have you heard a student say of an assignment, "I can't be bothered" or "It's a waste of time"? Somehow, such phrases have become legitimized in the student lexicon. They are cousin to "I prefer not to" (remember Melville's Bartleby?) and give off a whiff of arrogance, implying that the student, not the professor, is the better judge of pedagogy and purpose.

Students will find more significance in learning activities when they are fully engaged with the material. One of my teaching strategies to help them connect is to repeat important quotations or concepts, each time with a different emphasis or a bit more detail. Students who are fully attuned will find that they keep discovering some nuance that had previously been obscured. The material doesn't change, but the listeners will change, and suddenly, if they listen long and hard enough, they'll understand it at deeper levels.

I learned this strategy twenty-five years ago when I attended a lecture given by the Catholic theologian Hans Küng. His topic was the Reformation. Before he spoke, he drew on the blackboard nine concentric circles resembling the solar system. The smallest ring, he explained, represented where many of us stood with our limited grasp of the subject. Küng's purpose was to enable us to learn from his wider experience. This meant repeating many times the same points, but each time encompassing more information as he led us from ring to ring of understanding. Had he begun at the outermost ring, he would have lost our attention as soon as he started to speak.

If teachers do their jobs properly, their students' rings of understanding continue to widen during the course of their academic careers. What happens internally is what matters, for there's no rule that says clarity or understanding is the ultimate goal of an education, or even of a single class or assignment. Students are not on a journey to perfection; they are on a journey to completion. They need to be shown that the most significant intellectual growth comes through the process of engaging difficult material—not necessarily through mastering it. When students hear and really understand these words, it is as if a tight spring is released inside them; they relax, and they decide to enjoy the experience. Like an athlete who builds strength by flexing certain muscles, students bulk up their minds through the exercise of thought and inquiry.

Thus the choice to listen becomes a significant part of our thinking world. We can decide to genuinely encounter the material by listening to and grappling with it at a deep level—or we can decide to meet it superficially and come away with very little to show for the experience. Encourage your students, Kelly, to decide today that they are going to meet the material head-on and not let it overwhelm them. Remind them that they were given a mind to serve them but that, unfortunately, many people serve their minds by listening to fears or doubts or giving in to procrastination. "I can't do it" or "I don't understand this" or "This is too hard" typify their responses to difficult, demanding tasks. In most instances, I've learned, these are self-lies to rationalize a lack of desire. Students can choose to use their minds with energy and determination, or choose to avoid the complex or difficult, to be an active participant in their own learning, or to be detached from it and passive toward it. Students need to realize that they are not competing with other students or their professors. They are competing only with themselves and the content of the text.

4. *Take detailed, well-organized, clear notes.* My exams ask students questions that are based not just on memorization but on their understanding of their notes and reading assignments. Each day I open with a thesis or statement of purpose for that day's discussion and lecture. I ask students to listen for this thread and organize their notes accordingly and then review them shortly after class, filling in any material they didn't quite have enough time to write down or clarifying and grouping ideas while their memories are fresh. I appreciate that many of my students are auditory learners, and others are visual learners; and so although I lecture in depth, I also use the board, outlining as I go. Images, lists, or diagrams can also help students grasp ideas, and when used properly as a supplement to rather than a substitute for explanation, they can be effective teaching tools. Learning to take good notes is a skill that students can develop with a modest amount of effort and perseverance; the summarizing and processing that note-taking requires is still another way to get them to engage with the material.

Suggest also that students review their notes daily and ask questions at the start of the next class. Often I begin the day's session by asking, "Do you have any questions about what we've covered so far?" Studies of retention have shown that if we don't write down and review an oral message, we forget about 90 percent of the material within a week. Daily review will help students keep the material focused and organized. This will also help them on exams, when they may well be asked to reduce large quantities of material to a couple of pages—to what I call the "essential minimum." Here I think of *confluence*: what a wonderful word that is. It refers to those junctions when many widespread ideas, impressions, insights, convictions, and readings all run together like a series of streams into a river. This kind of synthesis will happen only if students stay on top of the material.

In his poem "Little Gidding," T. S. Eliot includes four lines that become a theme for my classes:

> We shall not cease from exploration
> And the end of all our exploring
> Will be to arrive where we started
> And know the place for the first time.

That is, when we reach the end of anything—a book, a movie, a class, a life—our minds, equipped with a whole compendium of knowledge, insights, and experience, can look back and fully understand the beginning. Such holistic hindsight is also true for students who have carefully assembled a body of knowledge throughout a college course.

This brings me to the subject of examinations. Especially in the humanities, essay questions can be a valid and valuable means of guiding students toward understanding both broadly and deeply. Essays require students to develop and sustain a critical argument. Students undertaking an essay exam must identify and outline essentials, subordinate details, and develop a sense of perspective. They must sort through and evaluate evidence and distinguish between fact and theory. Only essay exams (or next best, orals) can measure such things. Essay exams encourage us to respect our minds and to use them. But now it seems that many humanities teachers elect to use electronically scored objective tests, almost as if speed over thoughtful consideration, accumulation of facts over understanding, is all important.

I administered objective exams in all of my classes during my first year of teaching and swore I'd never do so again. One, for example, was composed of two hundred multiple-choice, true/false, and matching questions on Truman Capote's novel *In Cold Blood*, which we had spent two weeks discussing in class. As I now look over that exam, I see how trivial and even insulting many of the questions were. Students needn't have read the novel to answer most of them; CliffsNotes would have done very nicely. I also realized from this experience that the exam encouraged laziness in the students and, I'm embarrassed to say, in myself as well. For that is the main reason I gave it—it was easy to grade. A quick run through the scoring machine, a few (or many) clickety-clacks, and the numerical grade is recorded. No human interaction. No connection between my learners and my role as a guide to insights, understanding, critical thinking. No wonder this exam provoked irritation among some of the students. Just as injurious is the fact that I hadn't prepared the entire exam by myself. Parts of it came ready-made from a testing service whose growth has since become a triumph for the industry and a near disaster for the students it purportedly serves. In effect I was saying to them: "I'm relying on others to do my thinking for me. I don't have the time to evaluate your progress."

Kelly, I know that writing meaningful, probing essay questions— and then reading them carefully and marking them fairly and accurately—requires time, concentration, and effort. But it's worth it. If the questions you ask of your students grow out of the discussions they've participated in, the lectures they've listened to, and the reading they've done, the tests themselves become learning experiences that increase what students know rather than being mere gauges of what they don't know. Don't teach to the exam. Write the exam based on the teaching. This means that a week or so in advance, you might want to reflect on what you've covered and then find ways to facilitate students' expression of their understanding of the material. There are many ways to use exams well, and I'm sure you've found your own. Sometimes I like to give to the class twelve essay questions in advance, telling them that three will appear on the exam. The most valuable stage of the process, I believe, is the period of preparation, and it is heartening (as it was for me as a student) to find how much class members learn through that process. On occasion it helps to ask them to submit questions they would like to be asked. I may use a few, rewritten to reflect my expectations. I also find it helpful to sprinkle throughout the lectures an occasional comment such as, "This would be a great question for the next exam." Through these and other techniques, we can make exams a *part* of the learning process rather than a mere test of it.

Examinations are an inevitably stressful but important rite of passage. "Students need to learn how to jump hurdles," says Barzun.

"That is a recurring feature of life." But be sure when you write them, Kelly, that you really think about their purpose from the students' point of view as well as your own. Ask yourself, What can students learn through this experience, and how can I help them learn through guided application of their efforts?

5. *Organize your time.* Tell your students that if they think they don't have enough time to prepare for exams or complete assignments, they should come see you. Nobody *has* enough time for anything; we *find* the time. "Not enough time" is another of our culture's hoaxes. We always have the time for what is important to us. I believe, and I think you would agree, that television is a huge time robber. By age seventy, the average American will have watched up to *seven years* of television—much of it increasingly trivial. What does this say about the value we place on time?

Not long ago I visited the dormitory I had lived in during three of my four years at Purdue University. Those were blissful years of hard work, absorption in my studies, and a few active friends. As the only English major living among pharmacy and engineering majors, I learned quickly what dedication to studies really meant. Except for the occasional snap of a light switch or scrape of a chair or whispered voice, after dinner our hallway was as quiet as a monastery. The one television in the building, which most of us watched only while we waited for meals, was far away in the downstairs lounge. With a few exceptions, we knew that education and television are antithetical.

Perhaps you can imagine my disappointment when I visited my old third floor and found the environment to be noisy, crowded, and undisciplined as students strolled from room to room with little or no respect for another's privacy. Most disheartening of all is that every room had a television in it. I recognize a student's need for relaxation and escape from the pressures of intensive study. I also understand how important the social bonds one makes in college can be. When entertainment assumes precedence over education, however, the student is the loser in the long term. Encourage your students, therefore, to find for themselves a quiet area where they can apply themselves to their studies without interruption of any kind.

6. *Cultivate and keep an open, positive mental attitude.* We also have control over most of our feelings. Any moment in class, a student may be feeling bored (about the class), disenchanted or angry (with the professor), bitter (about an assignment), or annoyed (by something said in class)—but he or she is creating those feelings. In any situation, we can choose to give in to these feelings, or to rise above them and meet the challenge of the moment. In this area of human behavior Freud was right on the mark when he argued that our thoughts create our feelings, which contribute to our actions. This is why the ancients tell us that what we preoccupy our minds with comes out in our lives: "Guard your heart, for it is the source of life," and "As we think, so we are."

For students to benefit most from any class, I recommend that they arrive (if possible) at least five minutes early, review the notes from the previous class, and settle their minds in preparation for the lecture and discussion. I try to teach my courses as intensely, vigorously, and searchingly as I know how. By this I mean to say that I don't simply serve up aging views long since recorded on yellowing and curling lecture notes. I want students not just to absorb new facts but also to rethink what they already know for I, too, will be thinking and rethinking the issues before us. Invite your students to think hard along with you—and get everything that they can from the experience.

Kelly, these suggestions can help put a student in the right frame of mind to be open and receptive to learning. To germinate, a seed must be subjected to the right combination of conditions. So, too, can students prepare their minds to be fertile ground. One of the paradoxes of life is that we are called to commit ourselves before fully knowing what we are committing to. Commitment is based not on facts, but on desire. If we *want* to learn, we can. Intellectual, like spiritual, development is the responsibility of each individual. No one, no matter how skilled, can do the work for us.

Finally, help your students to know that although you may take the subject seriously, you do not take yourself too seriously. Together, teachers and students read the writings of individuals some of whom have more expertise and insight and think more profoundly and deeply than they do. There is much value in contemplating great works of the past. As the drama critic Peter Brook says: "To go to a museum and stand in front of a series of extraordinary paintings from several hundred years ago, or to re-explore a play of Shakespeare's, brings one back to the fact that neither you nor I or anybody alive—painter, musician, author, director—can today touch that quality. And that's very healthy—and humbling—for us."

Warm regards,

CHAPTER 7

Reading

Dear Kelly,

"Do you read a book a week?" a student asked me one day in class, a note of sarcasm coloring his frustration with the course's reading load. "No," I said, after a suitable pause. "I don't read a book a week. I read four or five books a week."

Usually, I wouldn't have responded so abruptly, but I felt that the other students deserved to hear the truth—because implicit in his question was an underestimation of the importance of books not just in my life but also in the lives of many of his peers. Until I was well into my teaching career, it hadn't occurred to me that reading was in need of defense. I've always looked upon it as a natural and indispensable part of life, calling for no explanation. Yet all too often I encounter students who can't name the last book they read for pleasure; and I'm always struck by how many otherwise handsomely appointed American homes have no books in sight.

I remember years ago one of my professors asserting that unlike the French or the English, twentieth-century Americans in general are not known as a book-loving people. I suppose this is still true. When talking over summer plans, for example, how many Americans discuss what they are going to do or where they are going to go, and how few describe what they are going to read? In 2004 the National Education Association reported that fewer than half of us over the age of eighteen now read novels, plays, short stories, or poetry, and only 56.9 percent have read any book at all in the past year. Although the number of books published annually and of superchain bookstores continues to rise, the size of the reading public steadily shrinks, and with it the pool of shared ideas, insights, and experiences that wide reading provides. I can't even begin to imagine how a nation of nonreaders will effectively communicate, solve problems, and engage with citizens within and beyond its borders without the reservoir of understanding and knowledge stored within books.

The reasons for this decline in reading have a lot to do with the dramatic shift in priorities and lifestyle since the nineteenth century and the engines of commerce and technology that now propel us forward. The causes of this shift are complex, but a couple of factors seem painfully clear to me. First, everything in contemporary society "discourages interiority," as Sven Birkerts says in *The Gutenberg Elegies.* The endlessly diverting electronic advances of our visual and aural culture—from radio to television, cinema, videos, CDs, CD-ROMs, video games, to the immense reach and scope of the World Wide Web—have diminished for many people the practice and pleasure of immersing themselves in books. Reading requires an inner silence that promotes contemplation and imagination; flashing images, a cacophony of music and voices, the frenetic soundbyte-length snatches of thinking that electronic media flourish on simply preclude the more methodical, accumulative, revelatory process that reading represents. If current trends continue, says George Steiner, the joy that comes from attending to a demanding text, mastering the grammar, memorizing and concentrating, "may once more become the practice of an elite, of a mandarinate of silences."

Certainly a major enemy is the stupefying incursion of television into the privacy of our homes, our gathering places, even our schools. If so many people didn't depend on the entertainment industry for their living, I would love to turn off all TVs for a year—and then see what happens. Our nation's once-a-year "Turn Off the TV Week" has met with only modest success, for good reason, considering the grip that electronic entertainment has on our precious leisure time. We all know instinctively that the medium should occupy a minor role in our lives, for students and teachers alike; and yet this attitude is hard to find in our wired—and now wireless—age. "Parents can no longer control the atmosphere of the home," writes Allan Bloom, "and have even lost the will to do so." For many families, television is a major player that leaves no time for anything or anyone else. Life is short. Time spent filling one's head with increasingly trivial programming and pointless information is lost forever, but more important, the opportunity to explore the interior and exterior worlds with the kind of depth and breadth that reading allows is lost too.

Like you, Kelly, and like many of your students, I'm sure, I grew up in gratitude to my parents for leading me into the world of books. My parents and grandparents and aunts were always reading, it seemed, and by their example they encouraged my brother and me to do the same. And so, in the solitude of our bedrooms or sunk into the cushion of the living room sofa, or in the backyard hammock on a lazy summer day, we had the privilege of reading uninterrupted to our hearts' content. Saturday morning was my favorite time because I could lie in bed until noon, deeply absorbed in a book—or late at night, lights off, snuggled under the covers with a flashlight and my latest acquisition from Junior Scholastic Books. My love for books grew as I did, and I was discovering in myself an irrepressible desire for learning.

For my tenth birthday my father built a bookcase. It ran the length of one of my bedroom walls, and I loved to rearrange the books on its three shelves. The Nancy Drew mysteries, the Hardy Boys, Robert Louis Stevenson, C. S. Lewis, Agatha Christie, Sherlock Holmes, science fiction of any kind, horror tales (M. R. James especially)—these were among the early books and authors that fed my imagination and took me out of my own life and into someone else's. The sheer pleasure of that transposition remained with me as I became an adult and found new and even deeper ways to read, understand, and appreciate books. Little wonder that reading and writing have seemed for many of us not a chore or even a luxury, but instead an inevitability.

How thankful you must be, Kelly, that you never accepted the command of culture, time, and information that TV wields over most American households today. Like your parents, mine didn't acquire a TV set until I was ten years old, and then they carefully monitored and limited my viewing. The television never became the center of our family's interaction or my play hours. It was purposefully placed in a room downstairs, in a faraway corner, away from our upstairs living space and our bedrooms and the dining room table. By contrast, in this age of multiple-TV-set families, I some-times wonder if anyone shares a meal or a conversation without the television blaring in the background. As a child in a home that did *not* focus on television, I so enjoyed reveling in my own imagination, in my own way of working and playing and thinking, I was indiffer-ent to the tube most of the time. I continue to be so today.

The decline in reading is also related to the spirit of the age—riddled as it is with real or imagined anxieties, with local or global threats, with a troubling present and an uncertain future. When people are afraid, many of them turn away from the solitude that reading requires and the interiority that it invites. They look outside themselves for answers, and distrust what they discover, what they might be challenged to do, what they may be invited to contemplate, what questions about themselves they might have to answer if they look inside. The irony in all this is that they are avoiding the very means by which fear can be overcome and order restored, and that is by recognizing and accepting the common humanity that is the focus of most great art.

To immerse one's self into a book is to submit to the authority of another, which is anathema to a culture in which individuality is valued and leadership often (rightfully) challenged. It can be intimi-dating to read hundreds of pages written by a man or woman who knows more than we do about a subject he or she has studied and researched for many years. And if we've been raised in an environ-ment not given to deep thinking, if our daily diet of conversation is limited to empty chatter and a studious repetition of gossip, then we feel uncomfortable with, even threatened, by erudition. Note, for example, the people in your life who divert most conversations away from becoming too serious or deep or speculative.

"Bookishness has been twisted somehow into freakishness," says Norman Cousins, and, indeed, deeply ingrained in our culture are negative connotations surrounding terms like "bookworm" or "nose in a book." The implication is that readers are "lazy, aimless dream-ers," says Anna Quindlen, "people who need to grow up and come outside to where real life is."

In fact, the opposite may be true. Those who read are very much in touch with life, in some cases, too much so. By way of illustration, early in the semester in all of my classes I talk briefly about Maya Angelou's memoir *I Know Why the Caged Bird Sings*—in which she speaks movingly about how reading changed her life or even gave life back to her.

When she was four, her parents divorced and sent Maya and her brother, Bailey, to live in the rear of a Stamps, Arkansas, store with their grandmother and uncle. No explanation was offered; no assurance was given. On many nights the two children huddled together, alone, and cried and wondered, "Why did they send us away?" "What did we do so wrong?" Later, Maya fell in love with the words of Shakespeare. As she says, the line from "Sonnet 29"—"When, in disgrace with Fortune and men's eyes"—was a state with which she felt herself "most familiar."

During the next few years, her sorrow was compounded by the indignities of racism, sexism, and, worst of all, at age eight the horror of being molested by her mother's boyfriend, Mr. Freeman. Her subsequent courtroom testimony led to his conviction and soon thereafter his mysterious death. So traumatized did Maya become that she withdrew into herself and, except for rare moments with Bailey, refused to speak. She simply adopted the sane response of silence. She lived in a cage of her own creation.

But Mrs. Bertha Flowers, a kind and discerning neighbor, sensed her pain and helped Maya open the barred door. She first left a book with the sad child, knowing she would read it out of obligation, and then, later, opened her own collection to the girl. Maya spent the next year reading voraciously—nonfiction, poetry, fiction, drama—trying to come to terms with the pain and rejection that she felt, trying to find some answers. As she says, "To be allowed, no, invited, into the private lives of strangers, and to share their joys and fears, was a chance to exchange the Southern bitter wormwood for a cup of mead with Beowulf or a hot cup of tea and milk with Oliver Twist." She read, and she waited.

Finally, almost a year after Freeman's death, she began to speak, and did she have things to say. She emerged from her cage and began to sing—through her own poetry and essays. Reading had helped her to keep sane and to find herself; it had shaped and nourished her inner life as a child. Reading had helped her to emerge without bitterness, without anger. Like the protagonist in Roald Dahl's *Matilda*, "She had learned something comforting, that we are not alone."

What my example is intended to show is the valuable role reading can play in enhancing our relations with others. By experiencing, even vicariously, another's pain or puzzlement or perspective, we broaden our insight into the human condition and deepen the level at which we think and feel. We learn what qualities and emotions and desires we share with others who, in culture or generation or outlook, may seem to be very far from us. In other words, we learn about not just what makes humans different, but also what makes them the same.

"You think your pain and your heartbreak are unprecedented in the history of the world, but then you read," says novelist James Baldwin. "It was books that taught me that the things that tormented me the most were the very things that connected me with all the people who were alive, or who had ever been alive." And such knowledge is essential in developing our potential for relating to others. Through reading, we can learn to be members, not just of our own families, but of the family of humankind.

Like young Maya Angelou, at some point in their lives all of our students will need a "4 A.M. book"—just as all of us need a 4 A.M. friend, some source of comfort, guidance, and stability we can turn to when the dark night of the soul seems too long and deep to bear. It's a book strong enough to help us past what's troubling us inside. "You'll never be so unhappy," I often tell students, "that reading will not help you." With book in hand, we are never alone. "Old books, like old friends," writes Michael Korda, "are always the best of companions."

Some of us don't know how hungry we are until we whiff a delicious meal. Some of us don't know how lonely we are until we meet that someone special. Some of us don't know how incomplete we are until we have a child. In the ninth grade I didn't know how intellectually empty I was, and how much my mind needed to be fed, until I encountered a book that answered that need—a need that neither friends nor good grades could satisfy. When a book speaks to us, the message doesn't leave; instead, it becomes part of us, remains with us over the years, affecting us in ever-changing ways. Like the growth rings of a tree, each reading adds more substance, breadth, and strength to our experience with the book, and the layers continue to grow and expand as long as we do.

Kelly, do you know the excitement of waking early in the morning and feeling a deep peace because of what you were reading the night before? What are your 4 A.M. books? Along with the Hebrew scriptures and New Testament of the Bible, one of mine is Thoreau's life-altering *Walden*—a book that I have always felt was written especially for me. I can vividly remember my first encounter. I was in the tenth grade and Mr. Trent was my teacher. He assigned the entire book to us, and for each chapter we had to answer a dozen questions. I still have the original text—covered with my underlinings and annotations—along with my handwritten answers to the questions and the final essay I had to compose.

At the time, I was carried away by Thoreau's call to simplicity, by his voice of reason and moderation. Here I found an alternative to the unhealthy pressures to conform that preoccupied so many of my peers. Here was a way to retreat into long, uninterrupted stretches of calm, far away from the incessant, gossipy prattle of the everyday world. Here in the sentences that I underlined I discovered something deeply personal and transforming and with them, I think, I first began to cull from books what pertains to me:

> I went to the woods because I wished to live deliberately, to front only the essential facts of life, and see if I could not learn what it had to teach, and not, when I came to die, discover that I had not lived.

> If a man does not keep pace with his companions, perhaps it is because he hears a different drummer. Let him step to that music which he hears, no matter how measured or far away.

> Students should not play life or study it merely . . . but earnestly live it.

And so on, image upon image. Even today, Kelly, I can't read these lines without feeling their profound effect on me. And my reading experience of the book has deepened with time. Thoreau had taught me how to withdraw into myself, an unassailable place where pettiness grows less insistent and less harsh, away from the unrelenting clamor of daily life.

My feelings of intimacy with Thoreau and his contemporaries are very much tied to my love of place, and this brings me to another possible explanation for why some people don't read. If they travel at all, too many do so just to get away or to be able to say they've been here or there. If you were to ask them how the trip changed them, or what they discovered about themselves that they didn't know before they left, they're at a loss for words. When I announced to someone that I needed to return to Concord for a week to complete a chapter for a new book I was writing, she said, "What for? That's why we have the Internet. You can do your research that way without the inconvenience or expense of travel." But it's the inconvenience of getting there that makes the difference. Life is not found on the bloodless Internet. Life is found in the place. To see something in its context is to see it for what it truly is at a given moment.

Perhaps it was inevitable that I would become so deeply connected to the works of New England authors like Thoreau. Given that I was born and raised in Amherst, Massachusetts, and that along with my parents and brother I traveled often to Salem and Concord, the specters of Dickinson, Hawthorne, Emerson, and Thoreau loom large in my reading history. My memory of pilgrimages to Sleepy Hollow Cemetery, and reading the epitaphs of eminent nineteenth-century American authors, is as fresh in my mind today as the experience was when I first visited at age ten; and each year when I return to my hometown, Author's Ridge is among my first places to visit.

One day I said to my summer class, "Well, I'm here, but my heart is elsewhere." Then I explained that after Nathaniel Hawthorne died on May 19, 1864, his wife, Sophia Peabody, and their children, Rose, Una and Julian, eventually moved to England, where Hawthorne had been U.S. consul in the 1850s. Sophia died there in

1871 and her daughter Una in 1877, and they were buried in Kensal Green Cemetery in London, where they remained for more than 130 years—far away from Hawthorne. In 2004 concerned individuals approached Hawthorne descendants and other officials to inquire about the possibility of reburying Sophia and Una in Sleepy Hollow Cemetery. On June 1, 2006, their remains were exhumed and sent to the States. Joan Deming Ensor, one of Hawthorne's four surviving great-grandchildren, said on the occasion, "It was a wonderfully happy marriage and they never wanted to be separated—his letters were full of longing when they were—and this is very fitting after the two have been apart for so long." The afternoon of June 26 when I was meeting with my class, the reburial had been accomplished. How I would have loved to be there. Such is the personal attachment we can develop for the authors and works we admire.

We all know that a love for books usually starts early in life. If your students come from homes filled with them, then I hope that from your experiences they will hear an affirmation of their own; if, on the other hand, they come from homes in which books were rarely seen, never talked about, and seldom read, and if they feel angry or cheated (as many of them will) by their intellectual void, then perhaps stories such as these will trigger their curiosity, encourage them, and even give them hope.

My students find much hope, for example, when Eudora Welty says in *One Writer's Beginnings* that "any room in our house, at any time of day, was there to be read in, or to be read to" and that she "cannot remember a time when I was not in love with them—with the books themselves, cover and binding and the paper they were printed on, with their smell and their weight and with their possessions in my arms, captured and carried off to myself." And in Lynne Sharon Schwartz, who says in *Ruined by Reading* that being a reader changed her life, starting "innocently enough," but then "it infiltrated. It didn't replace living; it infused it, till the two became inextricable, like molecules of hydrogen and oxygen in a bead of water." And in Anatole Broyard, who recalls in *Kafka Was the Rage* his life in the Greenwich Village scene: "It was as if we didn't know where we ended and books began. Books were our weather, our environment, our clothing. We didn't simply read books; we became them. We took them into ourselves and made them into our histories . . . Books gave us balance . . . Books steadied us . . . They gave us gravity." For these writers, their own passion for books has been lifelong and real. So it can be for your students, and so it can be for their children.

I encourage my students to read everywhere—on trains and in cabs, in the backseat of a car and on an airplane, in lines or in a waiting room, between classes or into the night—and to welcome vacations for the open-ended, unstructured time they will afford them to read without interruption. At dinner with friends, among the first questions I like to ask is, "What have you been reading?" And if I see a stranger with a book, I can't resist peeking to catch the title, or asking to know it. More than one interesting conversation has begun with that opening, for readers are hungry to talk with fellow readers about their books. But one time I saw a young woman reading a book whose title was covered by her hand. I peered closer, until I caught her eye and she held up the cover for me to see: *Inflamed with Desire*. As Twain writes on another occasion, "Let us draw the curtain of charity over the rest of the scene."

It helps to affirm in your classes that the partnership between reader and book is a unique and invaluable one and that no glowing computer or TV screen can replace the fundamental joy of holding a book in one's hands, opening its cover, and escaping into its pages. "Of all the inanimate objects, of all men's creations," says Joseph Conrad in his autobiography, "books are the nearest to us, for they contain our very thoughts, our ambitions, our indignations, our illusions, our fidelity to truth, and our persistent leaning toward error." We can reread them, at our own pace, and reconsider what we've read. Unlike films or television or desktop computers, books are convenient, durable, portable, self-sufficient; they can be read or carried anywhere; they can be ingested slowly in quiet solitude; they are available to everyone. "The convenience of the book . . . will ensure a long life for it," says Robertson Davies, "unless we bring up a race that has forgotten to read."

And so, Kelly, you can do your part to encourage a new generation of readers by creating a subtext for your classes. Ask some of the larger questions that your own passion for books addresses: How do books shape and nourish our inner lives? What motivates readers to turn to books in this era of cyberspace? What role do collectors play in the preservation of books? What are the central issues for publishers whose business is the book? What will happen to us as a people if we become a nation of nonreaders? By leading your students through the answers to these questions, and many others, you will give to them an alternative voice to the indifferent ones they hear much too often in society.

As teachers, we are called to show the way to a rich and colorful and limitless reading life. Norman Cousins calls the book "the finest portable university known to man." I agree. It's never too late to enroll. Where reading is nurtured, insight, knowledge, and love will bloom. As our minds grow, we are able to help others grow. The Chinese put it best: "A book is like a garden carried in the pocket."

Hold onto your books. They will help you through. Let them be your best friend, and they will remain a solace in your life as they continue to be in mine.

Warm regards,

CHAPTER 8

Under the Spell of a Novelist

Dear Kelly,

Forgive me for not answering sooner. I was delighted as always to hear from you, but felt some trepidation when I came to the part of your letter asking me to say "something original" about Barbara Pym that you might draw from in the classroom. As a day became a week became a month, and as you patiently waited for my reply, I began to feel much as I had felt thirty-five years ago as a graduate student: what could I possibly say about the novelist's life and work that hadn't already been said more eloquently by others? It seemed I could never read enough or work hard enough or know enough to have any original insights into a subject about which I cared so much.

But your request deserves a response, and so like any good academic I turned to the best sources I could think of—the author, her work, and her readers. With your indulgence, I'll let the latter do my speaking for me, for they can describe in great detail and from many perspectives an experience we all share: what it means to fall under the spell of Barbara Pym.

When those of us who love literature begin reading a novel, we are invited to enter the mind of another, to allow our own world to be subsumed by the author's created one. In so doing, at times we are touched within by some sort of awe or joy or delight. We feel lifted. We feel transformed. We feel more fully and pleasurably alive.

Philosophers call such flashes of intense insight "aha" moments—as in *now I see, now I know, now I understand.* Christianity has called them "epiphanies"—from the Greek *epiphaneia,* meaning "a manifestation." Virginia Woolf calls them "moments of being," and Wordsworth calls them "spots of time."

Whatever name we apply, once they occur and we have considered them afterward in calm reflection, we also see that our understanding has fundamentally changed: the world is put into clearer perspective; we feel ourselves in touch with the rhythm of life in a fresh way; we begin to move in a direction different from anything we'd ever imagined, a direction that we know is right for us.

This describes precisely how many of my students and colleagues respond to the novels of Barbara Pym. Why? What is it about this particular author's temperament and work that casts such a powerful spell, one that draws us in so quickly and holds us so tenaciously? Why is it that for so many of her devoted readers the novels serve such a deeply personal purpose? Why does Philip Larkin's assessment of her books—"No man can read them and be quite the same again"—ring so very true?

Perhaps some clues may lie in the web of circumstances that led to my publishing, in 1987, a collection of essays devoted to this author. Maybe considering why Pym and her work have remained so vital and relevant throughout the years since her death in 1980 will help our understanding. In any case, I hope that my thoughts here will not only prepare ground for a lively, perhaps even Pymish, correspondence with you, but also shed a little light on the intricate, powerful, and wondrous kind of magic only Barbara Pym could create.

I'm sure that you remember where you were and what you were doing when you fell under her spell. Perhaps, too, you have considered at times how different your life would have been if you had not, on such and such a day and at such and such a time, opened one of her books—and begun reading.

Hazel Holt tells us in her biography of Pym, *A Lot to Ask*, of arriving in London as a new employee at the International African Institute where Barbara Pym also worked. Because Holt was an English major, the fact that there was a novelist on the staff was naturally expected to be of interest to her. But the title of Pym's book, *Some Tame Gazelle*, together with the name of the institute, somehow gave Holt the idea that the book was about big game hunting in Africa, which "was very much *not* my cup of tea." Only when someone lent her a copy did she undertake the task of reading it, and then, of course, she was "enchanted"—enchanted enough to become the author's devoted friend and tireless literary executor, and to write and speak and edit on her behalf ever since Pym's death.

Like many admirers, I wandered into this author's magnetic sphere through the recommendation of a friend. It was a rainy weekday evening in the summer of 1980, and I was on sabbatical in London—caught in limbo-land between a completed project and no project, between relief and letdown from which I hoped the attractions of travel abroad would help me to emerge.

The little I knew of Barbara Pym was through the writings of others. Early reviews on both sides of the Atlantic of her posthumously published *A Few Green Leaves* praised it as "charming and funny," "beguilingly comic," "magical," and "one of her best." Paul Bailey referred to the "quiet confidence of its unhurried narrative." These items, and others, I had clipped and inserted into a "back-burner" folder, along with Pym's photograph, which I had found in the *Observer*. I would later write that this photo revealed the sort of gentle, intelligent face we expect to see in wise, kind teachers, reflecting an unselfishness and a patient endurance—a face, in fact, not unlike my own mother's. And I had kept the obituaries I'd read from the previous January, notices that expanded my awareness of Pym, at least in the abstract, and planted in my mind the thought that here was someone I should look into.

Adding to my interest was the rapt enthusiasm of a friend who that night loaned me her copy of *Excellent Women*—still my favorite Pym novel. I read it straight through, and as I did so, to my surprise many of my distractions fell away, I felt assured, and I was filled with a unique sense of peace and warmth, an impression so intense that it seemed to expand into an ineffable joy that remains with me to this day. At the time, I didn't have the words or the understanding to explain such a strong reaction, but I did know I felt impelled to read everything by her and about her that I could find.

Sometime between that fateful summer evening of 1980 and the fall of 1984, increasingly drawn both to explore and to pay tribute, in a small way, to the ever-growing interest in her work in both

England and the United States, I began to form the idea for two books—a collection of original essays on her life and work, written by those who had known her or her novels; and an annotated bibliography of secondary writings in which I would trace how the work, once it had left her hands, had been received and interpreted by scholar-critics and contemporary reviewers.

In one of my classes, you may recall, I related how I researched and compiled the reference guide, but here I would like to revisit some of the steps by which I brought to completion a book titled *The Life and Work of Barbara Pym*, and in the process what I learned about her, myself, and her readership. Perhaps some of what I say will encourage you in your own work on the author.

You think you are alone, and then you look up, and you are surrounded. When I began work on the project, I was struck immediately by the enthusiastic way everyone I met or wrote to welcomed everything having to do with Pym—even when I knocked at their door without warning!

Selecting the book's contributors, for example, was a fairly nebulous process—a blend of instinct and coincidence and luck. I began by contacting those writers with whom I was personally acquainted, then reached out to others I had read or knew of. Sometimes one person led me to another—as my colleague John Halperin did for the novelist Penelope Lively and the critic A. L. Rowse; as Pym's friends Bob and Virginia Redston did for Gilbert Phelps; and as Constance Malloy did for Janice Rossen, who, I discovered, lived a mere thirty-minute drive from my home, was a reader at the Huntington Library (where I also had a desk), and was herself writing a book titled *The World of Barbara Pym*. A chance meeting with John Bayley on the occasion of his wife Iris Murdoch's talk at the University of California, San Diego, resulted in the wonderful opportunity to ask whether he would like to contribute. "I admire and enjoy her so much," he said. "I'd be very glad to do you an essay on her."

I envisioned having twenty contributors, but expecting that some would decline for perfectly understandable reasons, I wrote to thirty-five. Indeed, even the negative responses were revealing. "Although a keen student of Pym," said Auberon Waugh, "I do not feel I know enough about her to contribute." Lord David Cecil wrote: "I would have been pleased to write for you, . . . but, as a matter of fact I am nearly 82 years old and already committed to as many projects as I can possibly manage in the near future; so, regretfully, I must refuse." Philip Larkin, who allowed me to republish the introduction he had written for *An Unsuitable Attachment*, declined writing a new essay: "You mustn't think of me as a scholar," he wrote, "just a hack reviewer." And although John Braine, also a fan of Pym's, died three months before he could complete his promised essay, he gave a tantalizing glimpse into what he would have written when he said in an early letter: "I will give you an essay that only another novelist could write of his contemporary."

In the end nineteen of the group I'd contacted did deliver, and John Halperin's letter accompanying his piece typifies their feelings: "You have hit me in a vulnerable place: I love Barbara Pym."

A real challenge for any editor is how to arrange the essays in a collection like this, but in this instance the pieces, as they arrived, began to suggest three broad categories: "The Life," "The Work," and "In Retrospect." As my authors corresponded with me and submitted their work, I began to realize that my own strong response to Pym was in no way unique. She seemed to touch, to guide, to inspire us all.

One of the highlights for me during this period was flying to New York City the first week of October 1984 to visit the office of Pym's U.S. publisher, E. P. Dutton. There, I was allowed the immense pleasure of reading through four file drawers of reviews and other materials, with permission to copy anything I wanted to help with my projects. I also attended a commemorative tea at the Gramercy Park Hotel honoring Hazel Holt and Pym's sister Hilary on the occasion of the American publication of *A Very Private Eye* and, afterward, met with them in their hotel suite to discuss plans for my book.

I carried away from that meeting the pleasant memory of a very Pymish moment. As I was leaving the hotel room and just pulling the door closed behind me, I heard one of my hostesses say to the other: "Such a nice young man. So unlike the *other* American we met this morning." I can only imagine what Pym might have made of that scene.

As I reflect, it's hard to put into words the sense of excitement and good fortune I felt about working "with" this author during those early years. Here I was (as you are now), six years out of graduate school, seven years into my teaching career, and so privileged to embark on fresh and fascinating territory. Now, the early 1980s and its accompanying flood of interest in the Pym canon all seems a distant memory. But I also realize that in ways I will perhaps never fully understand, that early work brought me closer to Barbara Pym herself.

Robert Frost describes his reaction to reading one of D. H. Lawrence's poems in these words: "It was such a poem that I wanted to go right to the man that wrote it and say something." That was my thought when reading *Excellent Women* for the first time. Unfortunately, I couldn't go right to Pym and say something, for she was already gone from us. Luckily, though, I could benefit from the experiences and memories of those who had, and as they shared them with me, I began to see her more fully as a person, not just as a writer.

As you have already discovered, Kelly, sometimes when we fall for an author through his or her works, our expectations are disappointed when we actually meet that person. Not so with Barbara Pym. My correspondents confirmed how happy they were that meeting her only enhanced, and did not diminish, their regard for her as a person. "She had that wonderful combination of quiet charm and good manners that made you feel she really wanted to talk to you," wrote one. Another said, "In meeting Barbara one never felt that she had missed out on any part of life." It is this ideal that impressed another of my correspondents when she wrote of her one and only meeting with Pym. It had occurred only a few months before she died, and it elicited this description:

> I liked Barbara so much and I am so sad for you, that you never met her. She was so easy to talk to—thoroughly nice, relaxed, not tense, with no "side" at all, no desire to teach, or impress, or talk too much, or

dominate the conversation. In fact, she was, if anything, a little quiet and shy, though not really reserved, and didn't at all mind all the questions I plied her with! . . . We chatted easily about all sorts of quite ordinary things, from gardening to books. . . . She was a "lady" in the nicest sense of that maligned word. She had an inner glowing depth, and warmth and vitality. . . . I thought I would see her again before long and be able to ask more, but I didn't realize she was already ill, and that we would not meet again.

Yes, Barbara Pym was gone, but certainly not forgotten; and this brings me to my third and final point of entry into the nature of her amazing spell: it has not just endured, but has in fact grown to affect more readers with every passing year.

"No reputation is more than snowfall," says the American poet Delmore Schwartz. "It vanishes." True for some writers, perhaps, but thankfully Barbara Pym is an exception. Her literary reputation is secure; her books continue to attract a growing audience as the years pass; and the critical interest is ever-widening with, at last count, thirty-one books, many hundreds of essays, and forty-four dissertations as well as translations into French, Italian, German, Dutch, Portuguese, Hungarian, and Russian. Here I embrace the absolutely basic definition of "criticism" that Frank Kermode gave when he called it "the medium in which past work survives." As long as somebody is examining a piece of art, through whatever lens, it is surviving. Many of Pym's readers identify with the work, enjoy the work, and want to go on enjoying it. And critics continue to find new depths to mine there as well.

Certainly her appeal to the reading public lies partly in her fulfillment of the most fundamental requirements of any great writer: she is a storyteller, a teacher, but above all, an enchanter.

Do you remember your first reading of *No Fond Return of Love*? When I open it and begin to read, within minutes I feel an odd excitement up my spine and I am drawn into the comfort and relaxation of Pym's complete and credible world, where ordinary things suddenly become profoundly significant, where a new face is an occasion for speculation, where the pleasantness and security of everyday life dominates, and where only small crises—such as a fainting literary editor or a vicar gone missing from Easter services—form a counterpoint to that comfort. I know of few other authors who are able to describe an event, a room, a thought, a person, with such tangible and finite detail. We *know* the kind of person who earns her living as an indexer. We *know* how to behave when the rector comes to tea. We *know* what a macaroni and cheese casserole signifies. We *know* what makes a good jumble sale. We *know* who goes where for tea and whether they prefer seed cakes. Thus the everyday becomes extraordinary. "In minute, breathtaking ways," says Lisa Schwarzbaum, "Pym sizes up the harms, the conventions, the pleasures, and the perversities of small lives and bestows upon them the rare beauty and clarity of her own genius." Beneath the calm surface of her novels, the events of Pym's fictive day *do* make an imprint. When we close one of her books, we realize that nothing momentous has happened outwardly, and yet she has made us *care* for her characters and the minutiae of their lives. She helps us, as the decidedly un-Pymish William Blake once phrased it, to see the world in a grain of sand.

But I believe there is another reason for her staying power, and that is, through her books Pym meets us at our point of need—not only for pleasure but for companionship, for stability, perhaps even for consolation.

I have heard of numerous instances in which people grieving the loss of a loved one (or of their own health) have found comfort in these novels during their blackest hours. I know a married couple who got through a personal tragedy by reading the novels to each other every night. Paul De Angelis, Pym's American editor, has related how his reading of *Quartet in Autumn* "coincided" with his coming to terms with his father's death; and John Bayley has said the novels "not only sustained but calmed and satisfied" him "as nothing else could" as Iris Murdoch died slowly and cruelly from Alzheimer's disease. "All honest thought is a form of prayer," Lance Morrow has written, and Barbara Pym's honesty can lead us to a kind of Benedictus within.

I think this phenomenon occurs in part because her plots and moral clarities remind us of the importance of staying connected with others and, ultimately, with hope, with a simple faith in the durability of the human spirit. Her books, Robert Liddell writes, "often seem to come to us like gifts of nature, like the air we breathe or the water we drink (but purer and more wholesome)." I agree with your observation that Pym stays soothingly far away from the easy, sweeping nihilism of many twentieth-century writers. She reminds us, as did Henry James more than a century ago, that every life is a special problem that is not ours but another's. "Content yourself," James once wrote in a letter to Grace Norton, "with the terrible algebra of your own."

This is not escapist literature but "the kind of reading," says Lance Morrow, that "one does to keep sane, to touch other intelligences, to absorb a little grace." And we all could use a little of that at one time or another. I'll always be thankful, for example, that I had the sense to introduce my mother to *Some Tame Gazelle* when she was in her late sixties and facing some of the inevitable challenges that come with age. "It was the best thing you could have done for me," she said years later.

Pym's humor as well as the crystalline calm of her prose helped my mother to get through the ten times my father went into the hospital for surgery. During the first three of those in-again, out-again years, she busied herself with the novels, and over the next five years she took to heart Pym's solution to her own mind-numbing trials—"I just went on writing," she said. "It was all I ever wanted to do." Under her maiden name, Frances H. Bachelder, my mother wrote an essay titled "The Importance of Connecting" for my Pym anthology and a novel, published in 2000 under the title *The Iron Gate*. One evening, after she had spent a long and uncertain day at my father's hospital bedside, I found my mother asleep in her chair at home, a copy of *Some Tame Gazelle* opened on her lap. "I've been looking at this book again," she said, upon awakening. "I can't help it. It's just so funny."

But we need not be in our seventies or eighties to fall under Pym's spell, nor do we need to be suffering to appreciate the many possibilities of the text. Her words speak, I believe, to anyone at any age and in any state of mind who is willing to slow down and listen, because Pym is writing of the human heart. The context may be different from our own, and on the surface the characters may be quite unlike us, but the human heart remains a constant. Here, too, she meets us at our point of need.

The world in which Barbara Pym's characters live, whether urban or provincial, is the antithesis of ours in a significant way. Our world devalues those who make time to listen to the inner self; our society often equates the need for solitude and introspection with laziness, inactivity, and unproductiveness. We should therefore not be surprised to find that many people have lost possession of what Emily Dickinson calls the "appetite for silence." At work and at home, among friends and at play, there seem to be ever-lessening opportunities for quiet time. And as people grow older and their lives become steadily more hectic and fragmented, they find themselves caught up in a race against time, with no time to be alone—and silent. "The world is too much with us," writes Wordsworth; "late and soon, / Getting and spending, we lay waste our powers."

But Pym's is a quiet world, evoked in such detail as to make the reader feel that the action could not take place in any other milieu. These novels invite us to slow down, to retire within ourselves, to remove ourselves from peripheral concerns and the pressures of a madly active culture, and return to the center where life is sacred—a humble mystery and miracle. It is this ideal reader, I believe, that Joseph Epstein has in mind when he writes of those who "seek in fiction news of the inner life, who seek solace, who seek the pleasures of a superior imagination at work on the materials of everyday life." Barbara Pym's novels meet that need.

What, then, finally accounts for our attraction and devotion to Barbara Pym? Indeed, what makes her spell so captivating? The answer, I believe, is found in an experience I had many years ago that I enjoy sharing with my students.

As a youngster of ten or eleven, I loved to explore for an hour or so before suppertime several miles of woodland behind my boyhood home in Amherst. Before setting out on my journey, however, I always turned on my upstairs bedroom lamp. As long as I still saw the light, I knew I could find my way back.

One day I ended up in an unfamiliar area, farther than I had wandered before. All at once it seemed the forest had grown dark and convulsive with shadows. The air was thickly oppressive. Worse still, I couldn't see my bedroom light. No matter how I turned, I had lost my way, as if I were trapped in some dark corridor that endlessly twists and turns and doubles back on itself. My heart was thumping like fireworks.

During previous journeys I had always been disappointed to hear my mother's voice calling for me because that meant it was time to stop what I was doing and return home. But now I yearned for that sound, and when I heard my name called, faint but audible, I ran in its direction. Before long, there appeared the chimney, the tiled slope of the roof, finally the main body of my brown shingle-board house with its green shutters, and shining from the second floor window, a bright light. Within minutes, and with an enormous sense of thankfulness, I had found my way safely home.

Since childhood, my mother's voice has been an undeniable presence in my head; since 1980, so has Barbara Pym's. Most of her devotees say the same. "That's how it is with Barbara," says Hazel Holt; "once you've read the novels, she is with you forever."

More than her brilliant storytelling or unforgettable, gently quirky characters, more than her penchant for quotation or impeccably intelligent humor, Pym's greatest gift is her voice—a voice that is speaking directly to us, in private, in its own distinctive, soothing, and enthralling way. Unsentimental and wise, the voice behind the characters in these novels beguiles us early and will not let go. In her company, we feel safe. And although no amount of academic study will ever explain why we love one writer's voice above another's, we do know, says John Le Carré, that "partly it has to do with trust, partly with the good or bad manners of the narrator, partly with his authority or lack of it. And a little also with beauty, though not as much as we might like to think."

So, Kelly, that's what I think it means to fall under the spell of Barbara Pym, and once there, we want to return, often, to grow closer to this gentle and genteel sensibility. That's why we continue to read and reread her. That's why we attend conferences and produce books and essays on her and talk about her with our students and other readers. And that's why Eudora Welty wrote in 1982, "Quiet, paradoxical, funny and sad, [Barbara Pym's novels] have the iron in them of permanence too."

Warm regards,

CHAPTER 9

Life vs. Art

Dear Kelly,

You say that some of your students object to the character flaws of assigned authors. You shouldn't be concerned, for learning to read literature well inevitably leads to lessons about being human, some of them unpleasant. Once I spoke in class about Thomas Hardy's neglect of his first wife, Emma Lavinia Gifford. I argued that these facts, dismal as they may be, should not diminish for us the pleasures to be had from reading *Tess of the d'Urbervilles* or *Jude the Obscure*. One student said, "Why are we reading something so depressing by somebody so unpleasant?" I responded by quoting Chekhov: "Great art is never depressing."

The sad fact here is that the untrained mind will look for any excuse not to pay serious attention to the beauty of the object that an artist produces. If the creator stumbles, then we need not read the work. Following that line of thinking, let us remove from our houses all the works by writers and musicians and artists whose lives have included acts of selfishness, weakness, dishonesty, and betrayal. And then let us reflect on how impoverished our inner lives have become in the absence of these voices that can tell us so much about ourselves. The image in the mirror is sometimes difficult to behold. Perhaps those who judge the images of others most severely have within themselves the most to hide.

Kelly, the more we learn about authors' lives, the greater the chance that we will encounter some detail we don't like or approve of. But this ought not to destroy our respect for their greatness as artists or seriousness as thinkers. When we let personal biography take precedence over artistic achievement, Donald Greene wrote, "it distracts or excuses us from paying attention to what is the only reason for [the artist] being remembered at all—the fact that he has a great deal to say to us, in remarkably effective language, concerning matters that are and will continue to be of prime importance to the human race."

During my most recent trip to Hull, England, I visited the newly refurbished home of the late Philip Larkin, and it brought full circle cherished memories of my acquaintance with the poet. I can say without hesitation that my respect for his artistic achievements has grown, not diminished, the more I have learned about the man. Not everyone feels this way, however. As details about his private life were revealed, some of those who knew Larkin primarily from his published writings were appalled or disgusted to see how often his correspondence contained revelations of his complicated love life, his penchant for pornography, and moments of racism and sexism. If there is a theme that runs through many of the critical responses in England since the publication of *Selected Letters of Philip Larkin* in 1993, it is in effect, "We thought Larkin one of the greatest English poets; how he deceived us!"

Could Larkin really have been as bad as all that? Even if he was, does it matter? Of course not. Martin Amis said as much in a pre-emptive defense in the July 12, 1993, issue of the *New Yorker*: "The reaction against Larkin has been unprecedentedly violent, as well as unprecedentedly hypocritical, tendentious, and smug. Its energy does not—could not—derive from literature: it derives from ideology, or from the vaguer promptings of a new ethos."

I encourage my students to step away from ethos and toward a more informed literary perspective by focusing sympathetically on Larkin's unhappiness and to come forward with reasons that both the letters and the life—with their revelations of unsuspected foibles, weaknesses, inconsistencies, and faults—should not seriously diminish our admiration of the poet's gift. An artist's first duty is to be true to himself or herself; Larkin had a perfect right to reveal to selected friends the depressing or disturbing aspects of that self, just as he expressed its humorous or kind or sympathetic facets.

Although my students, most of whom are coming to Larkin for the first time, are removed from his world and may not share his obsession with death or his sentiments toward aging, marriage, children, religion, or the church—they have respect for his writing, enjoy his humor, and admire his honesty. In short, we can learn to respect, and maybe even to love, those who challenge our assumptions—especially if we perceive in their work what John Bayley calls "a saving grace." And Larkin certainly had the latter. He worked magic with words that most of us can only envy; Clive James astutely observes that Larkin "made misery beautiful." That alone is testimony to the redemptive power of art. The effect of the musician Sidney Bechet on Larkin is exactly the effect that Larkin can make on a reader coming to him for the first time: "On me your voice falls as they say love should, / Like an enormous yes" ("For Sidney Bechet"). Encouraging our students to hear that "yes" is the greatest tribute we can pay.

My first encounter with this poet occurred in 1967, when as an undergraduate student at Purdue University, I had been assigned to read and report on Kingsley Amis's novel *Lucky Jim* in the context of the so-called Angry Young Men. I noted the dedication page of that book and asked my professor, "Who is Philip Larkin?"

With enthusiasm he loaned me his copy of *Jill*, and that led to *A Girl in Winter*, then to *The Less Deceived* and *The Whitsun Weddings*, and much later to the essays and reviews. Here was a refreshing alternative to so much contemporary poetry that seemed at times too abstruse or too specialized or too private to be understood. Here was a poet who spoke directly and beautifully and often amusingly about subjects that—even as a youthful undergraduate—I recognized and cared about and thought about.

Not that I always understood what I read. "A poem can communicate before it is fully understood," says T. S. Eliot, and I think that was my experience. I was nineteen at the time, had never been to England, and knew little of English life and literature apart from what I'd read or heard, and so no doubt I missed the full effect of all sorts of references in Larkin's poetry that came from his milieu. The American critic Jenny Joseph has written of a similar experience when reading the "enticingly referential" poetry of John Ashbery: "Although an English person knows that the richness is there," she says, "I feel I'm getting slightly out of focus, blurred when it is particularly exact."

Moreover, what devices for "unlocking" poetry I had acquired came to me primarily by way of our study of the modernists—Yeats, Pound, most especially Eliot, who wrote in 1921, "The poet must become more comprehensive, more allusive, more indirect, in order to force, to dislocate if necessary, language into live meaning." Because modern life is complex and difficult to grasp, that argument runs, the poetry that conveys it must itself be complex, even impenetrable. But that perspective also helps to explain why many of us continued to read Larkin during our college years and carried him into our graduate study years. We could savor the richness without struggling with the obscurity.

Certainly the culmination of my admiration for the man and his work occurred when I was able to meet him, first in 1982, and again shortly before he died, in 1985. In 1980, upon learning of my consuming interest in twentieth-century English literature, Eddie Dawes—a professor of biochemistry at the University of Hull, chairman of the Library Committee, and fellow magician (an interest we've both held since childhood)—asked whether I would like to meet Philip Larkin. Dawes said he knew him and that they worked together on the university's library committee. "Although Philip is a shy man," he wrote, "it should not be too difficult to set up a dinner party for you to meet him."

Two years later I was able to return to England, and I had that opportunity at the home of Dawes and his wife, Amy. The event was completely stage-managed by Dawes, who had suggested to Larkin that he come to the house for a brief private performance of magic. Larkin was wary and shied away from the thought that he would have to discuss his poems, but Dawes reassured him. He arrived promptly at 7:00 P.M., conservatively dressed in a dark suit and tie and carrying a brown briefcase in which he held copies of some review articles that Dawes had requested on my behalf. Having driven himself, he complained how he had almost lost his way. He sat down, had a gin and tonic, and then we enjoyed one of Amy Dawes's splendid dinners of fish, vegetables, white wine, berry pie, and coffee. Afterward we moved upstairs to the magic room and performed a show for Larkin, including the three-card trick, which he took part in himself. The next day he invited me to his office, where he left me alone for an hour with his archives, and I noted those items from English journals that I didn't have, which he promised to copy for me. When I told him that I had in mind an annotated bibliography on him much like the one I had done in 1978 on Kingsley Amis, Larkin looked up quickly from his desk, pointed to his copy of Barry Bloomfield's 1979 bibliography on the writer, and said, "Sounds like a super-Bloomfield." I left Hull the next day.

Of that evening Dawes has said that Larkin "was kind enough to refer to it as one of the most remarkable he could recall." What I didn't know at the time but later learned from reading Andrew Motion's biography of Larkin is the effect our visit had on the poet. "More remarkable still," Motion writes, "in view of his certainty that poetry had deserted him," was the fact that as soon as we left Hull, Larkin wrote a short poem:

> Long lion days
> Start with white haze.
> By midday you meet
> A hammer of heat—
> Whatever was sown
> Now fully grown,
> Whatever conceived
> Now fully leaved,
> Abounding, ablaze—
> O long lion days!

"No matter how unassuming the poem appears," Motion adds, "it reminds us that while Larkin grumbled about his sixtieth birthday he kept faith with his work, recognizing and enjoying the fulfillment of his talent."

My last visit occurred three years later. In July 1985, at lunch with Kingsley Amis, I learned of the seriousness of Larkin's cancer—something Dawes had alerted me to in an earlier letter. When I mentioned that I was going to Hull, Amis said, "Surely you don't intend to see Philip." I said I hoped to, but he shook his head, saying he wasn't well. (Much later I learned that neither Amis nor his first wife, Hilly, had ever seen Larkin's home.) My wife Patti and I traveled to the Dawes's home not expecting to visit with Larkin, but that morning Dawes called him, and he invited us over. We arrived at 10 A.M. and relaxed for an hour in his Newland Park home. He apologized that his companion Monica Jones couldn't come down for she wasn't well. He sat in his chair, with me to his left and Patti on the couch with Dawes. Larkin was hard of hearing but spoke with great interest. He thanked me again for the show three years before and said he had been so moved by it that when he returned home he had written about it in his journal. "I should show you what I wrote," he said, but the opportunity never developed. Next he asked how the Barbara Pym book was coming along, to which he had contributed an essay. And we talked about Kingsley Amis, about whom I was also writing at the time, and I mentioned that I would love to show Amis my magic, too.

As the hour drew to a close, Dawes took out his camera and Larkin sat between Patti and me on the couch with an arm around each of us. He drew Patti close to him and said to her—she was twenty-five at the time—"You could be my granddaughter." Patti took to him right away; afterward I asked her impressions, and she said, "sensitive and vulnerable." Like me, she was much moved by the gentleness of the man, and the melancholy.

The flashbulb didn't work, however, and so we went outside and there took the picture that I later reproduced in an anthology I edited. Under my arm I carried a copy of *All What Jazz* with the inscription: "From Philip Larkin in the shade to Dale and Patti in the sun (temporarily and permanently, respectively, we hope)." A day later he called Amis to encourage him to see the magic show.

"We're all very excited about seeing your magic," Amis said to me the next morning over the telephone. And so yet another dinner party was set up, followed by a show—this time at Amis's home, and all because Larkin had followed up on my comment the previous day. I have since learned that Amis retold the story of how I had met and entertained Larkin, always with humorous embellishments.

Motion tells us that as Larkin grew older, "he was more inclined to show each of his correspondents the face he knew would please them most." Every one of the thirty-seven letters I received from Larkin—some handwritten, many typed—bears his stamp in various ways, by turns warm, humorous, helpful, self-deprecating, generous, poignant, and always encouraging—someone with whom I wish I had spent more time, someone to whom I wish I had written more often. For he always answered my letters, and apologized when he delayed in doing so. Only later after I had read Anthony Thwaite's edition of the selected letters did I appreciate that Larkin's private correspondence was for him what someone has called a kind of consolation and healing. As he wrote in "Aubade," "Postmen like doctors go from house to house."

The earliest letter I received from him is dated June 9, 1981. Eddie Dawes had very kindly passed along to Larkin one of my books, and he wrote to thank me and say, "I see . . . that you have rather specialized in British authors of the Fifties, and hope it has not proved too distressing. I think you deserve a spell of Tennessee Williams." On August 25, 1982, he expressed "a deep sense of gratitude" for the magic show that Dawes and I had presented, and wrote:

> I have gone round telling people about it. My publisher asked me if I knew the story of the juggler and the statue of the Virgin Mary, which apparently ended with a deep and disembodied voice saying, "Don't call us, we'll call you," but I expect you've heard that. . . . Since our meeting, I have duly become weighed down with my sixtieth year, which all seems very odd. "Now of my three score years and ten, Three score will not come again," I remarked to our archivist, who replied (well, almost) "And very soon I'll be bereft of the ten singles that are left" (he is almost exactly the same age). So you see, poetry is not a specialism round here.

Upon hearing from Dawes of my marriage, Larkin wrote on December 21, 1983: "I hasten to offer my congratulations, if a bachelor's congratulations on such a matter are worth anything. At any rate, if you do come this way next summer, as you hint, I shall be delighted to see you both." About the appearance of his book *Required Writ-*

ing, he added: "I expect by now you will have heard of my collection of oddments. . . . The reviews it has had have been far too favourable; very soon someone will cut me down to size, and not before time."

University of Hull affairs sometimes entered his letters, too, as on January 5, 1983: "The University here has offered me the choice of having my arms or legs chopped off (professionally, I mean), and I am just composing my reply. It will probably fall to Eddie to hold me down." On March 19, 1984: "We had a sit-in here last week, and Eddie (who is my Chairman) came from compeering a conjuring show to help me patrol the body-strewn floors. I wish he could have made them all disappear."

On April 26, 1985, after I had expressed interest in interviewing him for a book I was writing on Kingsley Amis, Larkin replied at length:

> I feel uncertain . . . how far I should be able to help either you or Mr. [Julian] Barnes [who was also thinking of writing Amis's biography] in any practical way. I have never had much critical ability, and Kingsley strikes me as an above-average difficult case for comments of this kind. As for the personal side, well, without suggesting that Kingsley has any special skeletons in his cupboard I should be rather reluctant to do anything approaching gossip about him, if only because he might do the same about me one day. So you may find yourself in the position of trying to get blood out of a stone! However, as a magician, this should present no problems—to you!

On September 15, 1985—my last communication with him—I sent by overnight mail a letter asking Larkin if he would consider writing in support of my application for a fellowship to cover another trip to England, and he wrote by hand five days later: "Your letter arrived this morning with full honours of bell-ringing and receipt-signing. $23.00! That's a lot of money. I only hope this more humble communication will take less than a week." And regarding my application: "Well, all right, but *caveat emptor*—I will act if you are prepared to risk it." In that same letter: "I suppose I am getting better slowly, but the whole business has led to rather a crisis of confidence. To go through the ice of daily life means you can never forget how thin that ice is—you are always listening for the next cracking."

That cracking would come sooner than any of us could guess. On December 2, early in the morning, I was awakened by my wife's gentle touch on my shoulder and opened my eyes to hear her say, "Dale, Philip Larkin has died."

I can imagine the melancholy that those close to him must have felt on that day, and the totality of the loss they continued to feel years later. I know that I was filled not only with regret, but also with gratitude that I had had a chance to meet him, and that my wife had as well.

The American consensus is that Philip Larkin was a very good poet who knew how to say serious things about serious subjects. We don't read him as simply the crusty provincial grinding away about old rundown Britannia, nor are we distracted by the many cynical voices heard since Larkin died. He speaks to our condition. Some American scholars and critics may consider him a minor poet, but his work has touched countless readers in a decidedly major way. Encourage your students to hear what artists' *work* says to them—not to stop with what critics may pronounce or biographies and letters may reveal. You will have done both the artists and your students a great service.

Warm regards,

CHAPTER 10

Writing

Dear Kelly,

When Mozart was three years old he first sat down at his sister's harpsichord in the family house in Salzburg "to find notes that like one another." That became his life's work. I enjoy sharing this story because I hear in it a metaphor for the writer—who strives to find *words* that like one another.

We know that for most of our students, writing will not become their profession, but that's no reason for them to overlook the proper study and practice of it. Although many of them come to our classes well prepared and eager to learn all they can about the craft, many others come from environments in which its importance is all but negligible. Or they have had so many discouraging experiences in school that sometimes "Oh, I hated English!" or "That was my worst subject!" are among their first responses when we announce to them the subject we teach. Because our society has devised so many substitutes for the written word—from telephone to radio to television to film—some say that we risk reaching the point where normal writing ability will be as rare among college graduates as is proficiency in higher mathematics.

Ignore the cynics. Your challenge is to make each class a positive and enriching experience regardless of any inner obstacles or negative attitudes or societal trends the students might bring with them. Help them to awaken the dormant excitement that comes from choosing the right words. To fall in love with language, says Aristotle, and to discover our thoughts and then to communicate them convincingly and eloquently—nothing is more satisfying.

Encouraging your students begins with your own evident passion for the craft. Never let up, Kelly, in affirming the importance of well-written prose. Share with them the unspeakable happiness that you feel in front of your own work. Refuse to compromise on the high standards you have set for yourself. Assure them that you are teaching not from theory but from experience—your own as well as that of other, more seasoned writers. (Don't hesitate to mention the two books you have published, or the five you have not. Rejection, after all, is an important part of the process.) Remind them often that good writing requires skill, hard work, a keen ear, continued practice, and lots of reading. Tell them the truth.

A good way of stepping outside one's own language and looking at it objectively is to learn a foreign one. It is a fact, paradoxical as it may seem, that studying two languages makes mastery of both easier. Along with French (required in college for my major), I studied Latin in high school one hour a week as a noncredit class because my mother said I should do so. I've never regretted it. If your students are going into science or medicine or law, then a study of Latin is essential. If they would like to improve their understanding of logic, then a study of Latin is recommended. Along with the rigors and the subsequent discipline this study incurs, it will take them deep into the English language. "What can *we* know of English who only English know?" Kingsley Amis asks, famously. A host of English words have Latin roots and disclose their meanings by knowledge of their origins. Knowing about those origins as well as the evolution of the language over time is also a door that opens to new levels of understanding and expression for the writer. So, to the recommendation to study other languages, I would add another: that all students take a course that covers something of the history of the English language.

Yes, writing is difficult, but let your students know that they aren't alone in feeling its rigors. Behind every text there is a living, breathing human being who overcame his or her own challenges to bring the thoughts to paper. In English classes a study of an author's life is an expected part of the curriculum, but note how rarely our own professors of, say, economics or mathematics or history ever shared with us the lives of the writers behind their chosen texts. (How dull information can be when deprived of personality.) If I were teaching a history of mathematics, for example, certainly I'd want to relate the enormous struggles that Pascal or Pythagoras endured to achieve what we now so blithely take for granted. Or select any classic on economics: it didn't just pop onto the page. It may represent many years of haphazard, fitful, incoherent thought and discovery before its author hammered out a text of principles and examples that became assigned reading on campuses across the country.

With all there is to do in life, and with time in such limited supply, why would anyone want to spend even a minute writing? It's useful to raise this question, and then to lead students through some of the many possible answers in the hope that they'll discover their own. You and I know that people write to say something to others, of course, or to complete an assignment, or to create and clarify their thoughts. As Emerson observes, "A man [or woman] cannot write two or three sentences without disclosing to intelligent ears precisely where he stands in life and thought."

But we also write to preserve for future generations what matters to us now. Where would any of us be if our ancestors had rejected the craft out of laziness or apathy? What if St. Paul had failed to overcome his own dejection and suffering and doubts and had not buckled down to the immense job of composing his epistles? All Christendom would have been the poorer.

Writers also write because there rises from deep within, perhaps unexpectedly, something that they need to say to themselves. "The process of writing is always a healing process," Richard Rhodes reminds us, "because the function of creation is always, *always*, the alleviation of pain—the writer's first of all, and then the pain of those who read what she has written." Sometimes our writing is not only a message from us to others but also, from a deep place, a message to ourselves, something that we had not been aware of before but now need to consider. If our students write what they really know, they will tap into feelings and perspectives and insights that will enlighten not just themselves but their readers. Tell them to write from that place deep inside, for that writing is best that is most congruent with who we are.

To reach such depths the writer must call upon tools much more sensitive and complex than the pen or the keyboard. I enjoy telling students about my friend, the late Salvatore Salla, an Iranian artist whose portrait of the former shah and empress of Iran hung on one of the palace walls until the shah's overthrow. Salla and his wife, Trudy, immigrated safely to the United States and settled in San Diego, which is where I met them.

As Salla aged, palsy and other afflictions set in, but I noticed that his work grew ever more beautiful and vibrant and detailed. His wife rigged a brace to help steady his hand, yet I couldn't imagine how he was able to create such stunning portraits when burdened with such significant handicaps. When I asked him, he replied, "Ah, but I can still see!"

As an artist paints not just with a brush or oils but with the eye, so an author writes not just with a pen or a typewriter or a computer, but with the ear.

The American novelist Anne Tyler develops her first draft in long-hand on a yellow-sheeted notepad while she sits on the edge of her bed. When asked why she doesn't use a typewriter, she said, "Since I really do seem to do it by ear, if I'm typing I can't hear as well." She went on to explain that because she hears her characters' voices in her left ear, the clickety-clack of the typewriter would drown them out.

Developing the ability to hear words internally takes time and practice, of course, and it is especially difficult for those who haven't pursued an active reading life, for the more we read, the better we will hear the printed word. If I find in a student's essay an irrel-evant or incoherent paragraph or two, then I know that the writer hasn't *heard* the words. My note in the margin is, "Listen to your sentences." I suggest to such students that reading work aloud, to themselves or to a trusted listener with an educated ear, forces the writer to listen physically, which also encourages him or her to tune in to the language at a deeper cognitive level. The process of saying heightens the awareness of meaning; articulation requires reframing thoughts into words and more often than not clarifies both. Hence, when students read their work aloud, they should ask themselves, am I saying what I want to say?

I also find it helpful to set false deadlines. If an essay is due February 15, for instance, then suggest that students pretend it is due on the 11th and develop a polished draft by then. The extra four days will give them time to step away from their work, read it with fresh eyes, perhaps get feedback from their professor or another reader, and then rewrite.

Most composition classes, as you know, are more about revision than writing. James Michener once said: "I have never thought of myself as a good writer. Anyone who wants reassurance of that should read one of my first drafts. But I'm one of the world's great re-writers." Rarely do any of us get it right the first time. Rarely do we know what we're going to write about until we've completed a first, very rough draft. (All of my letters to you have taken at least three drafts.) Sometimes when reading a student's essay I'm at a loss to know its focus until I've reached the end, where I suddenly discover the central point or thesis. This tells me that the essay is a one-draft job.

Students need to give themselves permission to develop their thoughts without restraints. Instead of talking about their plan, they should just get it out on paper before they forget it—no matter how uncertain they feel or confusing it sounds. To talk about the work is to give it away, to weaken it, to take away its magic and its strength. Encourage them to write the first draft before they do any research. One of the joys of writing comes from discovering in what we have written something we weren't aware we knew. If students do their research first, they might never experience that joy. With time, they'll learn to trust their instincts. Even if they have no idea how something fits in, they should give themselves permission to include it; they can always toss it out afterward if necessary. Graham Greene once explained how he might introduce a character or an incident without knowing the point of doing so. Then thirty thousand words later, he suddenly realized what the character or incident had been doing there.

Although as teachers we work very hard to show students what power can be derived from a command of the written word, there will always be some who, out of fear, laziness, or misunderstanding, turn in work that is not wholly their own. Plagiarism is a growing problem at all levels of education, especially given the inestimable sources of ready-made texts on virtually any subject that are only a series of mouse clicks away on the Internet. For a set fee, a student can buy a paper on almost any subject. For no fee at all, they can cut and paste material into their own assignments.

If on the first day of class you set your policy, and if you select essay topics with special care, you'll go a long way toward reducing the likelihood of plagiarism. Just as a well-placed news story about the consequences of tax evasion works well before a filing deadline to discourage those who might be tempted to cheat on their taxes, so a story or two about the dreadful consequences of plagiarism will help deter someone who might be considering it. To ease into this, I assure students that I'm not questioning their integrity but fulfilling my obligation to educate them. Then I usually relate an experience I had during my first year of teaching.

It was early in November 1973, and as I was reading through a set of students' writing assignments, it became obvious to me that one of my pupils had copied his essay from another source. I didn't want to spend the time and energy searching for the source of the material, so the next day in class, I said: "One of you has copied your paper from an outside source. At the end of class if you come to me and tell me what you've done, I'll give you the chance to rewrite your essay. Otherwise, I'm afraid that you'll have to receive an F for the semester."

At the end of class, *three* students came forward. Apparently, revealing themselves was less costly than the price they'd have to pay for the misdeed itself. I gave them all a second chance, and I think they learned a lesson they never forgot.

If I sense that it's necessary, I stress the importance of integrity in all that students do and then tell of a colleague at a prominent university who was blackballed for life from academia after one of his graduate students discovered that he had plagiarized more than half of his doctoral dissertation. Another helpful reminder is to require that they attach a signed cover sheet to every essay that states: "By signing my name below I confirm that the attached essay is solely my work and that I have not consulted outside sources without the knowledge and permission of my professor. I fully understand the consequences of plagiarism." Not only does this codify my warnings, but also it asks students to take responsibility for their actions in a way that emphasizes honor and integrity.

In turn, to assure them that I respect the time and effort they have put into their assignments, I promise to read their essays twice. The first time, I do so without a pencil in my hand. I read to learn. Then I reread the essay as a critic, looking for places where I can offer suggestions for improvement. I tell students that I always try to view their essays through "university eyes," asking myself whether what they have written would meet universal academic standards and if not, why not. My feedback is intended to be constructive—aimed not at them personally, but at their work and always, I hope, written with a certain courtesy of heart.

Often as a child I accompanied my parents to the concert hall. My mother, an accomplished musician herself, could discern within minutes how much the pianist did or did not know of the composer whose music he or she was playing. "He doesn't know Beethoven" or "She understands Brahms' heart" typify her whispered remarks to me as we listened to the performance. Afterward, over dinner, we would conduct what our family called a postmortem—a detailed analysis whose purpose was not to tear down the artist, but to understand what worked and what didn't, and why. From this I learned valuable lessons about critiquing another's work, including that of my students, in a positive, supportive way.

You know as well as I how vulnerable young students can be as they are first developing, how easily they can be confused by conflicting or intentionally unkind opinions. Kelly, I wonder whether teachers realize that students never forget being humiliated. How unfortunate it is in any field when someone is told only of his or her faults or weaknesses, without any mention of his or her strengths. Comments on papers should always balance observations about what the writer might do better with what the writer has already done very well.

For some students, performance in writing—and in all their classes, for that matter—may be undermined not by poor skills but by unsupportive attitudes from significant people in their lives. Such students may be fighting battles on several fronts, struggling to succeed in the world of academia at the same time that they're withstanding assaults against it. "When are you going to take some courses that will be *really* useful?" or "How is that going to get you a good job?" or "What are you going to have to show for all that time and money?" are hard messages for both the student and the teacher to ignore. I encourage students who are dealing with such resistance to depersonalize those comments and remind them that it's always easy for people to judge those who are experiencing what they themselves are not. Our world assumes that to be happy, we need to accumulate more, do more, and that we should build our lives around acquiring, not intellectual growth and introspection. But self-absorption is indigenous to all study, whether it is writing, reading, or research, and such focus may indeed require a certain withdrawal from the world and material pursuits—at least for a while. There's a lot of pressure in our culture to consume and possess, but teachers need to encourage their students to challenge such limited goals and to forge more meaningful ones defined in their own terms.

So much of students' lives are spent in a place of intense concentration that it's easy for others on the outside to misunderstand or even resent them. Some students come from nonacademic families in which they are the first ones to seek a higher education. So although we can understand the source of the discouraging words, we must find a way around them. When others don't understand our endeavors, we must keep our purpose clearly in mind. We must stress the empowerment that writing well can provide, not just for classes, but for life. As one professor advised me on an essay: "Find a subject that interests you and that you know something about, and write. Don't stop for anything. Don't allow pressures or difficulties or trials or heartaches to distract you from doing what you need to do, and do it well. Don't let anything interfere with concentrating on your responsibilities to your reader. Above all, never give up."

Many years ago I had a student in a wheelchair who obviously suffered from a muscular disability. In seventeen weeks Lenny was asked to read twenty pieces of short fiction and one novel, and to write four one-thousand-word analytical essays and a twenty-five-hundred-word research paper. Through the semester he kept up with the work; turned in all assignments on time, neatly typed; and performed well on the exams with the assistance of a student aide, who I assumed was also helping him with his work outside of class.

One morning as I was walking past the library typing room I heard an unusually deliberate "tap-tap-tap" through the closed door. Curious, I peered through the window. Inside was Lenny, his wheelchair pulled up to a desk, sitting before a typewriter with a dowel rod in his mouth, painstakingly hitting each key as he prepared the final draft of his essay. What took other students two hours to produce took him three days. He completed the course and was one of four to earn an A.

During the semester, to help Lenny stay focused, I gave him a laminated copy of a miniature graduation diploma inscribed with his name. I told him to carry it in his shirt pocket throughout his education, and whenever he felt afraid or doubtful or discouraged, to look at it to remind himself of where he was headed. On commencement day there wasn't a prouder student than Lenny as he wheeled down the aisle to receive his degree in political science. As he passed in front of my seat, he smiled at me and waved his diploma in the air. I knew what he was saying: "I finally got the real thing!" The last I heard, he was working from his home for a computer firm.

Someone might ask, why didn't his teachers help him? Why didn't they let someone type the papers for him? The answer, of course, is that we did help him—by expecting of him everything that we expected of the other students. We encouraged him by supporting his belief in his dream, by focusing not on his limitations but on his potential. If a student like Lenny can achieve by overcoming great odds, what does that say about the potential—and the responsibility—of most of our students?

As teachers, Kelly, I think we can help all of our students by keeping in front of them the larger picture. Encourage them to see in their mind's eye the benefits of their study, the purpose behind the task, the rewards of the completed essay, for example, or the completed research project. Eventually, they'll know the joy that comes when the dream in their mind matches the reality they've worked so hard to achieve.

In writing, as in all endeavors, we often learn best by example. You asked who has influenced me most as a teacher and a writer. I would have to say my parents—my father for his wisdom and tenacity, and my mother for her creative inspiration. More than her love of words and dominant passion for books, there is her piano playing. I hear it in my mind when something I'm writing begins to gain momentum. I hear it as I walk to my classroom early each morning to begin a new day.

I started this letter about writing with a musical reference. I'd like to close with one, too, for the more I think about it, the more connections I find between the lyricism, power, and depth of expression inherent in the two art forms.

Like music, writing is about rhythm and timing and sensing your audience and seeing and hearing yourself through their eyes and ears. It's about anticipating. It's about becoming so locked into your subject that you can tell when a point needs to be reemphasized or when a question is shaping itself. It's about knowing, immediately, if the reader will follow the discussion, and if not, why not. Like the musician (or the lecturer, for that matter), the writer must be able to keep the audience continually in mind. Too often, students seem to forget the reader altogether, and so I like to suggest that they write their first draft as a letter addressed to an actual person. The nature of letter writing compels them to keep another person in mind. The writer who remains focused on the reader as a musician focuses on an audience is compelled to shape the product in such a way that it becomes clearer, more accessible, more fully realized. To write for another is to think through the message in new ways and, consequently, to express it from a more highly informed perspective.

My mother has played the piano all her life, and in her story I find some precious lessons that many students (and teachers) can learn from. Her father inspired her. As a child she learned to love music. "Only classical," her father had said, for he was afraid she would get into a lot of playing that "wasn't worthwhile." He wanted her to have a good foundation—just as we want to have our students well grounded in their chosen field.

Her father, himself a pianist and cornet player, knew not just the music, but tales of how the composers looked and lived as well as where and for whom they played; and so Mozart, Beethoven, Schubert, and Strauss all seemed like her friends by the time my mother started to take formal lessons at age seven.

Miss Turner was her teacher, remembered in my mother's inner eye as a sprightly lady, henlike—and very serious. On a typical day my mother was given a piece to study; she would go home, learn it, and then return a week later to play it for Miss Turner several times.

"That's fine, honey," Miss Turner would say, "now go home and practice some more." Dutifully, my mother practiced up to three hours every day after school, no matter how tired. So she would spend another week on the piece, play it for Miss Turner, and again she would say, "Fine, fine, now practice some more."

This would continue for several weeks until finally one day Miss Turner would say, "*Now* I think I can help you." In other words, my mother was in the hands of a first-rate teacher who encouraged her to do all she could on her own and then, and only then, did she offer to help. It's a principle I try to remember in teaching my own classes. You can best help your students only after they have given their full effort to the task.

When my mother turned fourteen, she wanted to study with Alistair Brown. After a distinguished career onstage and at the university, where he taught music theory for thirty-five years, he turned to private lessons: six students a year—that was all. His methods were exacting. He could be harsh at times, but the results were always notable.

"How wonderful to be a teacher," my mother said years later with the benefit of accrued wisdom, "every one of whose sentences conveyed something." Intense, passionate, serious, no small talk, everything Alistair Brown said meant something. If he didn't feel it, he kept quiet.

One day, after repeated requests by her father to take my mother on as a student, Mr. Brown granted her fifteen minutes. "Play your best for me," he said. "Fifteen minutes: no more." She selected two early pieces by Chopin. A week later, he wrote to her: "You have never seen my criticism of others in print. I won't do this for several reasons. In the first place the truth would shatter many. In the second place, I won't offer any criticism unless asked for it, and then I charge a lot. In your case, however, it's different. I won't charge you, but I hope you will pay attention."

My mother did pay attention. His full page of criticism was blunt and honest and of great value. It came from someone who had been everywhere, read everything, and heard everyone in his discipline. He spoke from experience. Most important, she had asked for it, and he offered it not in the public forum, but in private, and not out of spite, but out of a genuine desire to give direction. What a priceless gift.

She still has that letter. Of all that he had written, it's these words that she remembers best after so many years: "You know the notes, Frances, you understand the tempo, but you haven't learned to listen. You don't *believe* the notes. You're just creating pretty sounds. Play what you feel, and if you're really honest, you'll be playing for everyone else. Come back to me in five years."

My mother was cast down, but with her father's encouragement, that was the time she started to listen with new ears. When she turned nineteen, Mr. Brown indeed took her on as a new student. By listening to him about listening to herself, my mother grew as a musician and as a person.

Every student needs a mentor or two—and this, Kelly, is where you fit in. Present yourself early on as a tried and trusted individual who will be objective and honest, telling students what they need to hear (and not necessarily what they would like to hear), in a way that will do them the most good. If somehow I could have the good fortune to ask a world-class author one question, I would provide him or her two chapters of my best writing and inquire, "What isn't there?" Then I'd sit back and listen.

Happily, in Mr. Brown my mother found someone who knew

how to encourage and support while remaining firm and utterly honest. He had to be, he said, "Otherwise, I am wasting your time and you are wasting my time." As a teacher, I continue to aspire to be like Mr. Brown.

Each week my mother went to learn. She absorbed everything, but it took a solid ten years of slogging it out day after day before she began to find herself musically. Perhaps for that reason alone, to this day she is reluctant to criticize others in public. She knows how hard it is to take command of the instrument, to liberate the talent within, and to forge a partnership between medium and message that can carry the full weight of expressions of the soul.

Those who are successful in any endeavor are their own severest critics. In the back of their head is a voice that acts as a monitor and says from time to time, "Watch it!" "Are you listening?" "Be honest!" This is neither criticism nor arrogance, but instead a quiet confidence that comes after years of thinking, reading, experimenting, and pushing not just for the right phrase but also for the best one.

Finally, may I remind you that a huge (but often overlooked) bonus that comes from the teaching of writing is how we ourselves improve as authors from active work with other authors. I know that I write better and read better, that my sensitivities to the language have increased—in part because of the years of reading and responding to tens of thousands of essays written by students. Never lose sight of how much you can learn from your students, and what a gift it is to work and play with others in the magical—if sometimes maddening—realm of language. In guiding them toward the heights, we discover new peaks that challenge and strengthen our own capabilities.

Warm regards,

CHAPTER 11

Marriage

Dear Kelly,

I have found a passage in Jacques Barzun's *Teacher in America* that is rather relevant to something you hinted at in your latest letter—I mean, the haunting fear you hold of marrying wrongly, and that the choice might well sound the death knell for your academic career. Here is the passage: "How many careers have been broken near their beginning by the demands of some insensitive and possibly jealous young wife [or husband] of good family who 'could not see why John must work at those musty old papers every night.' Those who cannot see why will seldom accept an explanation, unless they are like Blake's wife, humble souls of different stations from their lord and master."

Regardless of their professions, most couples when they marry face enormous interpersonal struggles. Different cultures, different outlooks on the world, different challenges, different needs, different expectations—all of these can cause a rift that might seem at times unbridgeable. But bridge that gap we must, if it is our choice to share our life with another person. How? How can two people learn to live together and share their lives and continue to love one another? As the poet Rainer Maria Rilke wrote: "For one human being to love another is perhaps the most difficult task of all, the epitome, the ultimate test. It is that striving for which all other striving is merely preparation." We marry strangers; and it takes years before we see the whole person, if ever. I am sure that many couples would agree with Anne Morrow Lindbergh when she wrote in *Dearly Beloved* nearly thirty years after her wedding day: "Only two real people can meet. It took years of stripping away the illusions, the poses, the pretenses," and this is why partners must "never regret the past, call it a waste, or wipe it out."

Unfortunately, on many campuses there is a prevailing prejudice against combining family with academia, although from your comments I'd guess you're convinced they can, indeed, be combined. In any event, the conflict of interests between marriage and academia is much exaggerated. A son and two academic jobs works fine for my wife and me. We understand how the career path unfolds, and we both have found that our productivity has increased since marriage. Our work schedules are less strict and our flexibility is greater than those of friends in nonacademic positions. Other than meetings, office hours, and class sessions, we can choose where, when, and how to engage in our academic work and interests; and for a creative individual such as you, that is an ideal position to be in, with or without a family.

Nevertheless, your concern, Kelly, is certainly one that all truly dedicated teachers have shared. And although no other individual is identical with you, no other situation identical with yours, and therefore your choices are your own, I can observe that as academics we do share some commonalities.

Given the unique demands of our profession, I would agree that it's preferable not to marry early in your career but that if you do, it's advisable to marry someone in academia with similar or complementary interests and a firm resolve to make the marriage work. I credit most of the understanding I have in this matter to the example set by my parents, who had been married for sixty-one years when my father died in 2005. On this subject their example has taught me nearly all I know.

I once asked my father what most impressed him when he first met my mother. He described for me a day he walked into her office for a visit. "I'd like to talk, Stan," she said, "but I've got this work to do." Her devotion to her responsibilities connected well with my father's own early ambitions.

Certainly the deepest satisfaction of my father's life, apart from family, was his work as an academic, to which he gave the greater part of himself. My mother always understood this. "If your father's happy in his work," she told me, "he's likely to be happy in his home." Was she ever resentful of his devotion to his career? "I was *proud* of what he was doing," she said, "and I was just too busy to be resentful. I never felt neglected, never even gave it a thought. He was busy, and I was busy. To put it simply, I think I worked along with him, but in a different way." I suspect that my father's satisfaction was high, too, because he knew that he was appreciated and his work was greatly respected.

Theirs was a life of quiet domesticity during my parents' tenure at the University of Massachusetts, then Purdue University, and then the University of Maine where he served as president for twelve years, and they would not have had it otherwise. My father's increasing demands as an administrator and public speaker eroded their privacy a little, but he maintained it as best he could and remained a close friend to a few, a familiar name to many. "Ours was not a common marriage," my mother said. "Our travel and academic work made it more exotic, if that's the word. We both learned along the way, I especially." Indeed, it was an unusual marriage because of what my father did and what my mother learned. Work was the constant through their lives together; their tasks may have differed, but the goal of their separate labors was a shared one: a happy, productive life for their family and themselves. And this view was passed on to my brother and me.

Some friends with whom I have shared these insights into my parents' marriage have told me that they were uncommonly fortunate. Perhaps so, and yet as I reflect upon most of the people whom I have met through them, I find the same to be true for those couples, too. They married not because of family or societal pressure to do so, nor because of personal insecurities. They married because they found in one another a kindred spirit. "Academics played an extraordinary role as a source of talk between us," my father told me on the occasion of their fiftieth wedding anniversary. "We have had a terribly good time together, and we've not come to the end of our little adventure, either. We haven't finished talking."

In contrast to this domestic ideal, I remember my father telling me of a couple he knew early in his career. She was a professor of theology at a research-intensive university; he was a CEO whom she had met twelve years earlier in graduate school. During his acquaintance with them, he was struck by the husband's seeming incompatibility with his wife's temperament and interests. He was not by nature inquisitive, and seemed domineering and possessive. On several occasions my father witnessed his tendency to minimize her chances to talk and had been present in her office when he interrupted her with phone calls on trivial matters. She also told my father how her husband interfered with her work at home and expected her to perform many minor domestic tasks and errands he easily could have managed himself. In the ten years my father knew this couple, he never saw a book in the man's hand; his conversation was usually about himself. In short, he seemed like a gentle but manipulative tyrant who always made sure he got whatever he wanted. Where is it written, Kelly, that a husband has the right to impose his will on his wife—or vice versa?

What led her to marry him and then continue to accept what appeared to be a restrictive and distracting relationship for so many of her most fruitful years is not clear. They had no children, and she never expressed a desire to have any. She was financially independent. She wasn't a loner. One day after a long period of mounting disagreements, her husband said, "Either it's your work, or it's me." She walked out of the marriage.

The ultimatum speaks for itself. To strip another of his or her work is to strip away part of that person's soul. For this husband to demand that his wife should abandon the small voice of her unique genius was to ask her to betray her reason for being alive. The whole point of aspiring toward anything is to learn to give yourself totally to that endeavor; in that process, you find the best part of yourself and of your common humanity. In her case, from that point onward she knew there was one thing in her life she could rely on: her scholarship. It became her most necessary and exacting pleasure. No longer burdened by the accretion of stress and the depletion from demands, she chose to live quietly by herself, close to campus, and sustained by her love for books, her passion for her classes, and her remarkable gift for friendship. "I have no feelings of despair," she

wrote to my father six months later. "I continue to work, spend con-
vivial evenings with friends, and lead a comfortable life." She now
seemed, in Chaucer's words, "my own woman, well at ease."

Kelly, you are a woman of deep thought who holds in her grasp
something as important as breathing: the examined life, the life of
thoughtful reflection, the life of the mind and spirit. Your commitment to and passion for literature is woven into your being. It's part
of who you are. You are fortunate to have discovered a focal point
that fulfilled and guided you early on, so you've never felt like there
was something missing. You are also one of the privileged few to be
pursuing the life of leisure—meaning not that you don't work, but
that the work you do is work you want to do, work you thrive on.
I know that you don't take this for granted. I also know that to be
an effective teacher, you must be a thinker. That's what you're being paid to do. And that requires a lot of time alone, immersed in
silence, without fear of interruption or external demands. How did
Rilke put it? "To go within and for hours not to meet anyone—that
is what one needs to attain."

You realize, of course, that in this regard and many others you are
predisposed to swim upstream against a strong cultural current that
undervalues or openly scorns intellectual contemplation. A teaching
career, by which we really mean a life of the mind, is antithetical to
society and therefore antithetical to the expectations or experiences
of the majority of people. I remember after I had been teaching for
seven years. I'd published two books, was still single and living in
an apartment. A friend asked me, "When are you going to have
something to show for your life?" This is the same friend who, upon
learning that I had earned all of $1,150 in royalties for my first book,
said: "So that's what it comes down to. Four years work: $1,150."
Both times, I said nothing. What could I say? Her question betrayed
a naïveté I hear all too often, especially in regard to the sometimes
esoteric achievements of an academic career; in that view, the value
of one's life and use of time is measured by how much one has, ma-
terially, and by how much one earns. Because people with this view
don't *see* anything happening, they assume nothing is happening.
How fortunate I was to learn early on to calculate wealth in terms of

intangibles, with sacred relationships, books, and learning the central focus of my life.

Unlike the commercial world, the intellectual world that you inhabit operates quietly, in private, with its sometimes modest product made manifest many years later, if at all. You would no sooner produce a lecture or essay or book without time for incubation than you would produce a baby without gestation. Unfortunately, as I've said in a previous letter, many people have lost the perspective that comes with silence; instead, noise rules their lives, and their growing attention to it has crowded out other sensibilities. They are less observant, less thoughtful, less caring, less conversant, and therefore less human.

I should think that you would require in your life someone who is intelligent and unselfish enough to understand and respect your need for privacy and silence. The novelist Nadine Gordimer says, "I long ago made it clear to everyone, even those closest and dearest to me, that during my working hours no-one must walk in on me." Wouldn't you want in a companion someone who supports and understands this in you and yearns for it himself? Wouldn't you want to live with someone who is as committed and passionate about his research as you are about your own? Fortunately, you live in an era of choices; the societal pressures to marry and any stigmas attached to being single that were prevalent in the nineteenth and early twentieth centuries have been erased from most sectors of Western society. It is just as absurd to marry for the sake of marrying as it is to depend on another for your happiness. Stay focused on the work to which you have been called, maintain the integrity of your heart, and I can promise you that all in good time, you'll meet the person you need to meet. Surrender your worries. Don't decide before you have to. Until you meet such a person, luxuriate in the assurance when you awaken each morning that you can take possession of the new day in unquestioned liberty.

That advice, by the way, my parents gave me when I was in college and, like you, fretting about the seeming antipathy between life and art. On the one hand, I loved everything about my schoolwork, but on the other hand it seemed that all my friends were getting married, and I wasn't. Fortunately, not once do I recall my parents bringing up the subjects of marrying and having children. I felt absolutely no pressure in that regard, and for that I am grateful. Rather, they encouraged me to continue with my studies and follow my academic and cultural interests wherever they might lead. "You'll meet the right person when you become the right person," my mother once said. I didn't marry until I was thirty-six, and when well-meaning friends asked why I had waited so long, I said, "I hadn't met Patti."

Some people have a hard time believing this, but there's no professional competition between my wife and me. I think the reason is the three years of friendship when we were both starting our careers relatively early together. By the time we were married, Patti was headed for graduate school, intending to become a teacher and speech pathologist; I was seven years out of graduate school and eight years into my teaching career. I well understood the challenges she was facing and would be facing, and I encouraged and supported her as I'm sure she would have done for me had the roles been reversed. If she hadn't married a fellow teacher, in fact, I doubt she could be as positively self-absorbed as she is. Once when asked what she most likes about her professional life, she said, "I get to do what I want to do." And when I'm buried in my work for long stretches of time, or away at a conference or conducting research, she never complains. Yes, she misses me, but she also knows that the work is essential to my well-being.

You may recall my talking with you of Donald Hall's marriage to the late poet Jane Kenyon. "Loving to work" became their nature; although the two poets did not speak to each other all morning, "her presence in her own study," working on her poems, meant everything to him, enabling him to concentrate on his own. Had he married someone who preferred society and conversation, Hall admits, he would have wasted his time at parties. Solitude won out over company because their personal and professional relationship thrived on it. And so like them, for Patti and me and now our son—our lives are organized around our work, and we would have it no other way. The joy that comes to us from our absorption in work cannot be explained to someone who hasn't experienced it. My wife requires a lot of time alone, and so does our son, and so do I. We didn't marry in order to restrict ourselves, but to extend ourselves.

You ask what to be wary of in a marriage. Again, I feel rather out of my element to even comment. From my reading and from my observations of other couples, I'd have to say that more marriages are ruined by a need to control and a lack of genuine respect within the home than have ever been ruined by cruelty or unfaithfulness. Life can be troubling, for example, when one person is spending so many working hours wandering far off in an interior, intellectual landscape and the other is not. Estelle Faulkner never adjusted to her novelist husband's moods and closed-mouthed ways. "Without open communication between them," says Stephen B. Oates, "they both drank too much: Faulkner when he wasn't writing, Estelle when he was." And in her last years, Emma Lavinia Gifford, the first wife of Thomas Hardy, lived and died in two miserable attic rooms as her husband wrote *Tess of the d'Urbervilles*, *Jude the Obscure*, and other fine works in the study directly beneath. "He treated her with a cruel lack of understanding," says John Fowles. "You stand there and still feel the pain, their separate isolation, in those tiny upper rooms."

Nevertheless, there's a lot to be said for this much-besieged institution, marriage. I love what George Eliot has to say in *Adam Bede*: "What greater thing is there for two human souls, than to feel that they are joined for life—to strengthen each other in all labour, to rest on each other in all sorrow, to minister to each other in all pain, to be one with each other in silent unspeakable memories at the moment of last parting?"

In this regard I think of C. S. Lewis, who died in 1963, and of Joy Davidman, an American with two sons, whom he met for the first time in 1953 and married in 1956. We know from his letters that for Lewis the attraction was at first intellectual. Davidman was already a poet and novelist of some reputation, and like Lewis she possessed, says one biographer, "a formidably penetrating mind, a love of intellectual debate, and a contempt for sloppy reasoning." She was his equal in intellect and personality.

Although their short life together was much affected by her having cancer, those years of marriage until her death in 1960 were ones of complete fulfillment for Lewis. "I never expected to have, in my sixties," he said, "the happiness that passed me by in my twenties." Of the marriage Lewis's brother wrote that their home was "enriched and enlivened by the presence of a witty, broad-minded, well-read and tolerant" woman whom he had "rarely heard equaled as a conversationalist and whose company was a never-ending source of enjoyment."

I regret never meeting them, but if I had had that good fortune, I would want to ask them, What does it mean to live with a fellow author? What makes the arrangement work or not work, and why? How does life at home contribute to the creative process? What is the cost of a work of art or a caring relationship? In one way or another I suspect that most creative people have asked these and related questions.

Unfortunately, Kelly, there are no "how-to" books about the intellectual life within marriage. (Perhaps you'll end up writing one.) All you can do is continue to search for hints here and there in the letters and diaries of novelists, poets, biographers, scholars, editors, and collaborators; and read also their biographies and, if they exist, autobiographies. Seek out living authors, visit with academics, and learn from their examples. Above all, whomever you decide to marry, make sure that he has a compelling purpose in life and is willing to support you in yours.

Warm regards,

C H A P T E R   1 2

The Adventures of Scholarship

Dear Kelly,

"Whenever you feel passionate about an author," said the biographer
Matthew J. Bruccoli, "go ahead and plunge into the research. Don't
worry about what other scholars think of your project." This advice,
given years ago to a student of his fresh out of graduate school, I
now give to you with the hope that you'll make it the cornerstone
of your publishing career. Bruccoli's words are pertinent, I believe,
because you have decided with some anxiety to write your next book
on a living author. As you'll soon discover, the challenges will be
formidable, the discouragements will be many—but if you persist,
I promise you the result will be rewarding for many reasons both
personal and professional.

Like many of our colleagues, you and I lead double lives. Although
much of our energy is focused on exploring ideas with our students,
outside the classroom we are what Richard Altick calls "scholar-ad-
venturers." Our intellectual curiosity and our academic passion lead
us to delve into the literary documents and careers of authors we
admire. Part of that quest is the exciting dream most of us hold that
we will discover a fresh topic waiting to be explored. At least once in
my career, I had the good luck to find it realized.

In the summer of 1972 my father was in New York City to visit
with his friend Gordon Ray, president of the Guggenheim Memo-
rial Foundation, and during their conversation he mentioned that
I wanted to write my doctoral dissertation on Kingsley Amis, the
foremost English comic novelist of the twentieth century. Ray said
he knew Amis and would be glad to write to him on my behalf to
see whether he could set up an interview. I sent Ray a copy of my
proposal, and a few weeks later I received a note from him along

with a copy of Amis's response. "I'm sure you can imagine the mixture of tickled ego and slight sinking of the heart with which I read your letter," Amis had written to Ray in November. "Mr Salwak seems, from his dissertation proposal, a sensible enough young man, and he and I may get along together famously: but then again we may not." He agreed to see me for a minimum of a couple of hours' chat followed by lunch, "after which," his proviso stated, "I'm free to disappear from his life, but may well elect (and have the leisure) not to do so." If I was prepared to come all the way from California to London on that understanding, then he'd "very cheerfully" see me and do his best to answer any questions I may devise.

I wrote immediately, and on December 18 he replied with several possible dates and added: "Obviously, the sooner you can let me know which day is best for you, the sooner I can regard the other days as free for other appointments. But, with Santa at our throats, you needn't rush too hard." We agreed to meet at 11 A.M. on January 24, in his club, The Travellers', in central London.

His letter came at a crucial time for me. My dissertation proposal had met with some resistance—not surprisingly, considering that choosing any contemporary writer for such intense scrutiny would have been questioned in those days. One committee member had doubted whether the project was worthy, saying that he found it difficult to justify Amis as a fit subject "in the same breath" as, say, Milton or Chaucer. Another had advised me against writing on living authors. "It could not soon be completed," he said, "and research material will lead to endless further revision and revision." He suggested that I look for another subject—"the deader, the better."

But owing to the unwavering support of my director (who had led me to the topic in the first place) as well as Amis's positive response and my own consuming interest, I persisted—and two drafts later my proposal was approved unanimously. As I had argued, little of substance had yet been written on the man or his work, and so clearly this was an area wide open for exploration. "It's only a matter of time before someone steps forward to do so," I said. And given that most of Amis's contemporaries (including John Wain, Philip Larkin, Angus Wilson, Colin Wilson, John Braine, Alan Sillitoe,

Iris Murdoch, P. D. James, David Lodge, and others) were alive and still writing, I envisioned many years of fruitful research into their work as well.

When I left for London and that meeting with a writer who was very much alive indeed, I couldn't have known where the journey would ultimately take me. We travel outward to grow inward. To this day I can recall every feeling, every sight, every word, every thought from my ten days in the great metropolis on the Thames. I'd heard numerous stories about Great Britain's people and culture from my maternal grandparents, who were themselves English, and I had visited the city in the pages of more books than I could count. And so I was in love with London before I ever set foot there. That first trip marked an important turning point for me as a student of the world, and since then I've returned to that great city many times.

I arrived at the Travellers' Club ten minutes early and sat down as directed by the porter (whom I overheard say to an associate, rather indignantly, "He wishes to see Mr. Amis"). I did my best to relax, but I didn't know quite what to expect, nor did I know how a writer I so admired would receive me, although he had been cordial in his letters and over the telephone the day before. As I watched two club members pass by, I felt somewhat like the hero of *Lucky Jim* as he sees the notables of town and gown assemble before his public lecture and finds himself "admiring the way in which, without saying or doing anything specific, they established so effortlessly that he himself wasn't expected to accompany them."

Within seconds of Amis's arrival, however, I felt at ease and liked him immediately. He couldn't have been more courteous with his greeting. He stood about five feet nine inches tall, with hair a mixture of gray and sandy blond. He was wearing a dark brown suit, pastel green shirt, green striped tie, and—orange socks. There was no pretense or stuffiness in his behavior, and, in fact, after the interview turned out a success, he said one of his chief worries had been that I wouldn't be amiable. Apparently, he had had some unpleasant encounters.

We shook hands and he led me upstairs to what had been a television room. He chuckled. "The management would be quite upset if we were caught with a tape recorder," he said. "They frown on things like that." If anyone should come in and see it, he added, "We'll just stare at them and hope they'll go away. Possession is nine-tenths of the law."

Kelly, if you should ever have the privilege of interviewing an author whom you admire—and I hope you will have that opportunity, many times—it's essential that you do your homework before you meet. This means reading all that the author has ever published and as much about him or her as you can find and shaping your questions with care. You don't want to waste time during the interview by asking for information already available from other sources. What you're seeking is what is *not* in print—clues to his or her writing techniques or literary philosophy, or central themes, for example—and once you've fallen under an author's spell, you'll want to know everything. And oh yes, unless there are objections, bring with you a tape recorder and offer to send your subject a transcript of the interview for revisions or corrections before you use it. All this is my way of saying—respect the writer's time and talent. This approach has helped me find and reveal some new insight or understanding through many pleasant, stimulating, and enlightening conversations.

Over the next two hours Amis responded patiently and generously to what I asked. He spoke clearly, without hesitating, almost as if he had seen my questions before I posed them. If I had shut my eyes, I would have thought from his tone of voice that William F. Buckley was speaking. I have never met anyone so observant, humorous, and professionally thorough as he talked about his career, his novels and poetry, and closed with his thoughts on science fiction, criticism, and his life as a man of letters.

2:30 arrived: I had another hour's worth of questions, but it was time for lunch, and so we walked to the dining room where I enjoyed lamb chops, mashed potatoes, salad, potted shrimp, and a glass of burgundy, while he had ham, kippers, salad, and wine. I was so caught up in our conversation, trying to remember every gesture, every word, and every expression that I almost missed a brief but revealing event. At one point a friend of his came up to the table and asked, "Has the Rachmaninoff record arrived?" The reply was, "No." What I didn't know is that this was a code. Had Amis's reply been "Yes," he explained to me afterward, he would have used the interruption as an excuse to leave immediately—a method of safeguarding against the possibility of being bored by my company.

Conducting an interview is as uniquely rewarding as it is demanding. Given discipline, patience, and a lot of advance work, it may be the only means of really piercing the surface of a subject. It requires a giving out of everything you have and concentrating fully on what's being said and done. You want to make the most of the experience. To have only a few hours with your subject, as I did, makes the time very precious indeed. I didn't want to return home and think to myself, "If only I had asked that, or that . . . " The next morning I sat cross-legged on my hotel bed with a rented typewriter and transcribed the tapes. I felt exhilarated because for the first time in my young academic life (I was twenty-five), I was on the verge of making an original contribution to scholarship. During the previous day's lunch, Amis had called me, almost with reverence, a *scholar*—a high compliment indeed. I came to understand it then and know it now as a privileged position, hard-won. I felt legitimized as an academic and a professional.

We met again at the club on January 30 (on the tape I've sent, you'll hear in the background the clatter of plates and silverware as the waiters set up for a banquet), and I asked him another dozen questions followed by drinks. Before we parted, he promised to send me the proofs of his new novel, *The Riverside Villas Murder*, so that my dissertation would be up-to-date.

"My dear Dale," began his handwritten letter accompanying the package that arrived the next morning at my hotel. "Hope you get this in time. And that you enjoyed your trip. I certainly enjoyed our meeting, and very much look forward to more of the same when you're back this side. Good luck with the dissertation. Let me know if you find some annoying gap, anything not clear, etc. Or if you have further questions, etc." He signed it, "Warmest personal regards, Yours, Kingsley Amis."

The tone of his letter—friendly, courteous—foreshadowed the letters I would receive from him over the next fifteen years. Amis has written of his friend Philip Larkin that he was "always the best letter-writer" he has known and that "a glimpse of the Hull postmark brings that familiar tiny tingle of excitement and optimism, like a reminder of youth." May I say that I felt some of the same lift in my spirits each time a letter from London appeared in my mailbox with the familiar handwritten or typed address.

To get a publication out of a dissertation project early in one's career is a significant step forward. After *Contemporary Literature* accepted the interview for publication, I asked Amis for permission to print. A month later he granted it, apologized for the delay in responding ("due to twin pressures of work and laziness"), and sent along seventy pages of his novel-in-progress to be titled *Ending Up*. He concluded: "If I can be of any further help, don't hesitate to let me know; but you're well enough acquainted with me by now to realize that such a request, unless signed in blood, may not bring an instantaneous response. I hope all goes well for you, in your Amis project and in general." The interview appeared in the Winter 1975 issue, and I sent him a copy. "I must say I do seem to have gone on and on rather," he wrote, "but you must take the blame for asking so many answerable questions."

Once I was finished with my dissertation, *Kingsley Amis: Writer as Moralist*, I mailed him a copy and asked for his reactions. On October 17, 1974, he wrote: "Please forgive my remissness in not writing to you long ago. I thought your dissertation was very full and very fair, with an excellent sense of relevance and no wasted words. I can detect no substantial errors of fact, nor any material omissions." He concluded, "I remember with great pleasure our meetings in London." Though understandably proud of the work I'd done, I knew it wasn't close to being ready for publication (although I did send it to a few publishers after removing any telltale signs that it was a dissertation). Looking back on that early work fifteen years later, I said to Amis that I was embarrassed by it. "I'm glad to hear you say that," he said. "You didn't go far enough." I nodded. I had done my best but also knew that usually it takes many rewrites before a dissertation is ready for publication—as you, Kelly, have already discovered.

One of the joys of living contemporaneously with an accomplished novelist is that we never know what a new work will be like. The surprising publication of *The Alteration* in 1976—a wonderfully wrought what-if novel in which Amis imagines the world as if the Protestant Reformation had never happened—gave me another reason to write him, offering my congratulations and letting him know that I was sending a copy of my just-published annotated reference guide in which I traced the history of the reviews and critical responses to all of his published work. In August 1978, he wrote: "The book is very handsome and amazingly exhaustive. I feel both proud and slightly guilty at having occasioned so much hard work. And *useful*: this very week I must draft a blurb for my collected poems, due in the spring, and your record of the reviews of the earlier volumes will be invaluable. Many, many thanks." This meant everything to me. I had managed to please the person who mattered the most.

The spirit of collaboration and cooperation that exists in scholarship is unsurpassed, perhaps, in any of the other learned professions. As I grew and as my field of interest broadened, I felt confident enough to reach out to other writers, and here again Amis became a crucial link as he introduced me to John Braine, Colin Welch, Robert Conquest, Anthony Powell, and others. But in August 1978, after I had asked for his assistance in approaching John Wain (about whom I was by then working on a biography), he responded: "I feel a little leery, as I believe you fellows say, about approaching Wain on your behalf. For some years now there has been a *froideur* between us (entirely his fault, let it be observed), and my recommending you might do you more harm than good." He suggested that I write to Wain myself while playing down what I had done on Amis: "he isn't the sort of chap to be rude to strangers and I'm sure you'd find him helpful." As it was, Wain couldn't have been friendlier to me in his letters and, later, during our meetings at Oxford and in California.

The year 1980 approached, and I felt it was time for a follow-up interview on the occasion of the publication of Amis's sixteenth novel, *Russian Hide-and-Seek*. The Borgo Press had contracted with me to do a book for their series Literary Voices, to be titled *Interviews with Britain's Angry Young Men* and to include John Wain, John Braine, Bill Hopkins, and Colin Wilson, all of whom had agreed to be interviewed. In March 1980, Amis wrote: "I would be very happy to see you, update interview, indeed discuss any matter of interest within reason. . . . It will be fun to meet again." We chose to meet at his home in July. "Of course," he said, "if you'd care for a modest lunch under this roof my wife and I would be only too happy to have you. You're welcome to inspect the study where I'm writing this and where at the moment there are almost as many bottles as books." He added: "I hope you won't be too shocked at the renewed sight of me. I have put on a bit of weight and my face is a rather pouchy affair. We must arrange things so that you can't possibly mistake me for some relic of the previous generation."

Streets swelled with shoppers in the noontime rush hour at Hampstead Station. Rain speckled the pavement, and as I followed the housekeeper past a high brick wall, down some steep stairs, and into Gardnor House, the man who appeared in the entranceway—wearing a light blue sweater and tan slacks, with hair grayer than before and glasses —was a man I had no difficulty recognizing. "Well, you look no different than when I last saw you," he said, to which his housekeeper commented, "That's quite a compliment."

Narrow stairs led into a spacious and book-lined sitting room. A small dog nipped at my heels. Ever able to produce the well-turned phrase for any occasion, Amis said, "She recognizes origins of distinction."

Four years previously, after Amis and his wife had moved to Gardnor House, 4 Flask Walk, he had sent me a message: "Note new address; much more fun!" As we sat down I reminded him of that, and he laughed hard. No sound was more satisfying.

The room seemed to reflect its owners: hospitable, comfortable, and unpretentious. Absent was the earlier formality of the club scene; here was a more relaxed, domestic setting. Or so I believed. Through lofty windows I looked onto a pleasant garden, which, together with the house, had the air of being obstinately self-contained. Moments later we were joined by his brother-in-law, Robert Howard, and by Amis's second wife, the novelist Elizabeth Jane Howard—tall, stout, blond-haired. She settled comfortably in a chair, crossed her legs, and busied herself with needlepoint as we talked and sipped our drinks (scotch for Amis and me, vodka for Robert, nothing for Jane).

Thirty minutes later Amis looked at Jane, his light blue eyes shining perceptibly brighter, and asked, "Well, where's this lunch you've been promising us?" To get to the kitchen we had to walk through Amis's study. "I could do a lot of work here," I said. A 1960s Adler office manual typewriter (which would be sold a year after Amis's death in 1995 to a private buyer for £550) sat on his desk with a sheet of paper in its carriage. As I peeked at the words, Amis said he was writing the introduction to a collection of the essays of Peter Simple (a pseudonym used by the London journalist Michael Wharton). Behind his desk were three teetering piles of envelopes and papers and on a shelf a complete set of the *Encyclopædia Britannica*, a thirteen-volume edition of the *Oxford English Dictionary*, and other reference books.

The life that the Amises seemed to be enjoying in their new home smacked of an earlier, gentler era, and it was very English. The meal was a case in point: watercress soup, lamp chops with mint sauce, roasted potatoes, and red wine. Like my hosts, the housekeeper knew exactly what she had time for. Although I tried, I couldn't catch her serving me. As in a well-orchestrated performance, food appeared before me like magic; my wine glass seemed to refill itself. When faced with the decision of which dessert should come first, the cheese or the ice cream and apricots, the others deferred to the guest. "Let's save the cheese for last," I said. "Good!" Amis said. "Then we can have more wine with the cheese!"

In due course we were back in the sitting room. Once again he was an easy man to question, and forthcoming with his answers. He showed me the page proofs for his collected short stories, due out that autumn, and surprised me with a copy of *Russian Hide-and-Seek* with the inscription: "A wet but cheerful afternoon, 14th July, 1980. Kingsley Amis." (Its subject—a futuristic dream world turned nightmare—was at the time a far cry from the apparently contented domestic life that the Amises seemed to be enjoying.) And I caught a tantalizing glimpse of his famous talent for impersonations when he imitated a Soviet reviewer's attack on the book. Then Jane joined us and also signed her novel, *After Julius* (the one she had dedicated to Kingsley), with the words: "This is Dale's copy of my book, which I inscribe with my very best wishes." She then returned upstairs to work on some letters.

When Amis peered out the window, then leafed through a copy of the *London Magazine* "to find something to read," I understood this to be his polite signal that it was time for me to leave. We agreed to meet at 11:30 a.m. one week later at his new club, the Garrick; he had resigned from the Travellers' some years ago, he explained, because the Garrick, with its membership of lawyers, actors, writers, and artists, was more in tune with his own temperament.

"It was very nice for Jane and me to have you to lunch and we both much enjoyed the occasion," he wrote to me three days later. "You made an excellent impression!" He added that he had been talking with his friend Colin Welch of the *Daily Telegraph* who had said: "I saw a young American at the Kings and Keys who was not drunk with John Braine, who very much was." Amis said, "Dale!" Welch was astounded that Amis was able to identify me.

At the Garrick I had brought along my copy of a British scholar's book, recently published, about the 1950s poets, Amis among them. "It's nice," he said, "when somebody writes a book about you and your friends, isn't it?" He asked to see the book, chuckled, and said, "Let's see what mistakes I can find that your book can correct him on." In the next ten very entertaining minutes he had found seven factual or interpretive errors.

All seemed well in Amis's domestic life at that time, and I imagined a cozy scene of two fellow novelists working back to back in separate rooms of Gardnor House during the day, then reuniting in the evening and over a drink reading to one another their day's work. But then in 1982, I was surprised to learn that after seventeen years of an often stormy marriage, Amis and Jane Howard had separated painfully. He was now living in Kentish Town with his first wife, Hilly, and her third husband, Lord Kilmarnock, and for the first time in his professional career, he had abandoned a novel in progress. As I was in England at the time, I called him the next day and he invited me to come right over.

Hilly greeted me at the door, showed me in, and then left the room so that I could be alone with Amis. The change in his circumstances and appearance since 1980 couldn't have been more dramatic. His right leg was in a cast, he had a beard (which he said he planned to shave off when the cast was removed), and he looked dejected. Listening to him talk, I found myself wondering whether he would ever write a good novel again, a question that he may well have been asking himself. His confidence was understandably at low ebb. I abandoned any prepared questions, and instead listened as he talked about Jane, his club, and his stay in hospital.

We continued to correspond as I moved on to other projects, but the subject wouldn't let me rest. A recurring edginess and anxiety visited me whenever I glanced at my Amis collection or read a new novel of his. When Amis told me in 1985 that Julian Barnes had approached him about writing a book on his life and work, I said with interest and alarm, "Well, there'll be two then—one by an American." I was committed.

And so that year I began in earnest to revise my dissertation with publication in mind and asked for Amis's help. "As regards your dissertation, of course send it to me and I will read it through and comment on it," he wrote. Six more years of work lay ahead, however, before I felt ready to take him up on the offer. By then I was fortunate to have unrestricted access to his archival material, except for the Bodleian Library's collection of letters to Philip Larkin and Bruce Montgomery. Jack Gohn's 1976 bibliography alerted me to the Humanities Research Center's collection of Amis's juvenilia, his rejected Oxford thesis, and the notebooks and typescripts covering his first five published novels. Queries in *PMLA*, the *New York Times Book Review*, and the *Times Literary Supplement* helped me to locate letters held at Pennsylvania State, Syracuse, Princeton, and the University of Victoria. And when I learned that the Huntington Library might acquire the Amis archives for its collection, I spoke to the committee in strong support of the plan—successfully, for they bought the entire collection of almost one hundred drafts of Amis's novels, as well as various stories, unpublished plays, essays, notebooks, radio and television scripts, and 250 letters. Together, these materials span the entire course of Amis's career from 1934, when he was twelve years old, to 1990, and tell us much about his education, his evolution as a writer, his methods of composition, his friendships and acquaintances, and his respective tenures at Swansea, Princeton, Cambridge, and Vanderbilt. A gold mine, as it were, in my backyard.

I had no more preparation than this. I continued to exchange daily faxes with my editor at Simon & Schuster International, with whom I had by now signed a contract for the book, and I searched for photos as I completed and then revised a draft of the text. I had selected 1990 as my cut-off date—a pivotal year, to be sure, with Amis's ascension to knighthood in June, the publication of his twenty-second novel, *The Folks That Live on the Hill*, and the completion of his *Memoirs*. Then during the summer of 1990 and with my work nearing completion, I asked Amis over lunch if he would consider reading the first three chapters of my book because of their emphasis on biographical background. "Yes, of course," he said, "send them along and I will comment." I did so, and went on my way, pleasurably anticipating his response.

On October 10, 1990, I received back the chapters along with the following letter:

Dear Dale,

Thank you for letting me see the first three chapters of your book about me and my work, which I have at last read through with the attention they deserve. I return them herewith, marked here and there.

I am very sorry to have to tell you that I consider them altogether unsatisfactory. It is not that I find what you have written offensive in any way, or improper to its subject. It is that the level of your performance seems to me to be so low as not to earn a place on any serious publisher's list.

Please realize that no imaginable rewriting would rectify the situation. The fact that I have left many passages and pages of your typescript unmarked testifies to my weariness and boredom with them, not to their correctness or adequacy.

I think it would be best if the book were to be withdrawn.

Yours, Kingsley.

Imagine receiving that in the mail one morning. I felt baffled and downcast. Amis's response contradicted everything he had communicated to me in person and in letters over the previous seventeen years, and I was somewhat reminded of how I had felt in high school at the end of one semester when I received a couple of C's and one D on my report card, and suffered through the disappointment of my parents. (I brought my grades back up the next semester.) "All we expect of you," they said at the time, "is that you do your best," and I knew deep down that I had not.

But the Amis book was different: I knew that I *had* done my best, that my intentions had been honorable. But my performance had not risen to his standards—and that was a pretty hard knock. (Amis's biographer, Zachary Leader, would later write, "It is not clear whether he understood how brutal he was being in this assessment or if so whether he cared.") At the same time I was sure that Amis's objections were detached, not personal, and aimed at the text, not me—a fact confirmed by his agent, Jonathan Clowes, who wrote in a letter to my editor that the criticisms were "purely professional" and that "Sir Kingsley found Professor Salwak personally very pleasant and amiable." And although there's a very real possibility that my book was simply not as accomplished as I had hoped, in retrospect I believe that my editor and I made the right decision to push for publication despite Amis's objections and those of his agent. "One writes what one can," says Emerson, "not what one ought."

But for a brief exchange a year later, there would be no more letters between me and Amis, and I understood the shock of something being over.

Kingsley Amis: Modern Novelist was released by Harvester Wheatsheaf, a division of Simon & Schuster, in 1992. They published the book in part on the strength of positive reports from independent readers, including Barbara Everett of Somerville College, Oxford, who called it "a splendidly spacious, relaxed yet shrewd study of Amis' work. Lucid and very informative, it is ideally suited to the general reader." Others saw its merit as well, with several positive reviews, one calling it "mandatory reading for all students of Amis."

Three years after Kingsley Amis died on October 22, 1995, Zachary Leader, a professor of English at Roehampton University, was invited by Amis's son Martin and commissioned by HarperCollins to edit the collected letters from Amis. Over lunch one day I delivered to Leader copies of all of my letters from Amis—but one, the last one of October 1990. In July 1999, he wrote to say that he needed to raise a somewhat "delicate matter." Among the papers found in Amis's home was a copy of that letter to me of October 10, 1990. Leader acknowledged that the letter was "shockingly blunt," and although he understood why I had not included it among the collection I had given to him, he thought it should be included. Amis's literary executors had already deposited it at the Huntington Library, and it was available to other scholars. Leader also argued that it showed an important side of Amis—"how ferocious he could be in his later years." The letter, he continued, said "something about his willingness to sacrifice personal feelings for what he seems to have seen as the welfare of his reputation as a writer." Leader added that he had thought "long and hard" about the decision to publish and felt that, especially because of Amis's earlier warm and helpful letters to me, it needed to be included. With some reluctance, I agreed. As you know, Kelly, scholarship requires integrity—fidelity to the quest for understanding, regardless of where it leads. I suspect that in his own way, Amis was following something like that principle when he wrote that last letter to me (an explanation that Leader would develop in detail in his biography of Amis published in 2006). You, too, may face difficult decisions or harsh criticism or vehement disagreement at some point in your research and writing. Painful as these flashpoints might be, they are the sparks that ignite dialogue and inquiry; sometimes disagreement, not accord, advances knowledge.

Thus the "scholar-adventurer" sometimes follows paths and sometimes blazes new ones. In the study of literature, there are all sorts of ways to enhance the pleasure of an author's work; many extend beyond the primary act of reading it. You can read works of the writer's contemporaries. You can read into the history and culture of the times in which he or she lived and worked. You can read other writings about the author—biographies, monographs. And sometimes, you can meet the author, which can be a great treasure indeed.

When I say this, inevitably I think of my father, who all his adult life sought out people he was interested in meeting and learning from. I can recall, for example, the time he called me from New York with great excitement in his voice to say that he had just met Saul Bellow. Since his passing, great pleasure has come to me as I look through his book collection—and find many autographed by the author with personal greetings that testify to more than a casual acquaintance. Someday, perhaps my own son will discover a similar joy by going through my library of first editions, all personally signed by the authors themselves. Among them is a complete first edition set of Kingsley Amis's novels, poetry, and nonfiction, many of them inscribed to me.

And so yes, absolutely: if they are still alive and you have the ambition, I encourage you to seek out the authors you admire and, when possible, to visit and correspond with them. Collect their books. Learn all you can about their lives, their work habits, their attitudes. Write about them, and then bring that firsthand knowledge into class as yet another way of enriching the lives of your students.

Warm regards,

CHAPTER 13

Work

Dear Kelly,

Now that you've been practicing your profession for a while, you've come to see academic endeavor from the other side of the lectern. Yes, the ideals and attractions of the "community of scholars" concept are very inviting. But as you know, teaching can also be just plain hard work. I've thought a great deal about that aspect of the profession, and this has led me to some general conclusions that might prove useful to give to your own students while you strive to motivate them to do their best. You may also want to file them away for that time in the distant future when you find yourself contemplating the possibility of retirement and brooding about the unknown.

What is there to love about our work? Usually when people ask that, they are confusing the word *work* with *toil*, as in the biblical injunction after Adam's fall, "cursed is the ground because of you; / in toil you shall eat of it all the days of your life." But there is a huge difference between work and toil. Toil is the horrors of plantation slavery or the tyrannies of penal labor. Toil is the inescapable drudgery and meaningless activity of a nine-to-five routine or another shift on the assembly line that many people endure solely to earn money. Toil is the kind of soulless exercise that fosters what Joan Didion has called "the unspeakable peril of the everyday," and which many of us grew up determined to avoid.

But work, on the other hand, can be any meaningful, productive activity that not just supports our physical needs, but allows us to reach our intellectual and spiritual potential. Some people find genuine fulfillment in another day at the office or factory. Others are on the road or on their feet, providing services to support the health, well-being, and prosperity of their fellow citizens. For many of us, our work both in and out of the classroom is a source of growth and stimulation, an ever-changing challenge, a calling to be answered. Teaching revitalizes us, bringing health, contentment, or personal fulfillment; it gives us opportunities for sociability and companionship, fosters pride in individual creativity, creates a sense of personal identity, and stimulates wonder. Teaching enables us to use our gifts to their fullest and to direct our energies toward a purposeful task.

The attraction to the challenges of teaching grows early in life and stays with us, reaching its culmination during our latter years of formal education. Much like your experience, for me the five years in graduate school proved to be some of the most arduous study I've done in my life. But that's why I loved it so much. I discovered early on that my character was at stake: Was I willing to do the work? Could I meet each challenge? How far and how hard was I willing to push myself? Each day I felt that I hadn't read enough or learned enough or studied enough. I was up against better, more sophisticated and able minds. Always I felt underprepared, a feeling reinforced by a parable that one of my professors related one day: "Imagine that this blackboard represents spatially all that there is to learn about your subject," he said. "In a lifetime of concentrated study, with luck, you'll learn this much." Then he made a tiny chalk mark on the board, almost invisible to the naked eye from where I sat in the front row.

One student found the analogy so daunting, she felt it was reason enough to consider dropping out of the program. "If that's how he feels after thirty-five years of teaching," she said, "what does it say about my chances now?" But many of us found the professor's statement an exhilarating challenge to make the fullest use of the time we had. Happily, I accepted that challenge and have devoted fulfilling, if rigorous, decades to its pursuit.

I'm not exaggerating when I say that after all these years of teaching, I feel as if I'm just beginning. Like the blackboard surrounding that chalk dot, my chosen field is much too big and too difficult and too long for one life to fill. So much to learn; so little time to learn it. I treasure what the Japanese artist Hokusai says: "I have drawn things since I was six. All that I made before the age of sixty-five is not worth counting. At seventy-five I began to understand the true construction of animals, plants, trees, birds, fishes, and insects. At ninety I will enter into the secret of things. At a hundred and ten, everything—every dot, every dash—will live."

Each of us, student and teacher, must find his or her own way to the kind of self-discipline that empowers and invigorates us in our lifelong pursuit of meaningful, fulfilling work. For some, that dedication and focus comes naturally; for me, it was in part self-imposed. Like you, I loved what I was studying, but as a recent transplant from Indiana, I felt beckoned by the siren call of California's social and recreational vitality as well. To minimize these temptations, I drew closed the shades, turned on the answering machine, and called evenings my own. I attended classes in the morning and slept through the afternoon. My rule Monday through Friday was rarely to meet people after 6 P.M. All that time I devoted to my studies. I did this for four consecutive years. A Saturday afternoon study group of five others to whom I was accountable also helped me to stay focused and motivated. Dedication was cyclical: self-discipline engendered self-discipline. Hours seemed to pass like seconds. I was utterly happy, utterly unself-conscious.

Of course, as you too have discovered, such immersion in work is not without sacrifice. At times, I'm sure I wasn't the best of company among friends, for studying was my greatest enthusiasm. When a friend called in September to ask whether I could play golf, I said, "What are you doing in February?" (A few years later when he was in law school, he told me, "Dale, now I understand.") Personal relationships, too, can be made difficult or even impossible when one's energies are so directed, so single-minded. I don't know how married couples bear up—unless they're both going through the program together, as I mentioned in my earlier letter to you on the subject of marriage. To get the most out of the training, you must expend the best parts of yourself in your work and in your self; otherwise, you won't achieve the level you're capable of. Every instant I wasn't in class, it seemed that I was studying—in a fierce, determined manner. Now my students enjoy hearing of this, often, and so will yours.

As you know, Kelly, it doesn't matter if the work, whatever form it takes, is difficult or complex. You attack it anyway—and do whatever is necessary to complete it. For me, the task of engaging, understanding, and retaining difficult intellectual material meant rewriting my class notes, by typewriter then, and taking comprehensive book notes, and going over and over the material until I broke through to clarity. Some evenings I went into an empty classroom, stood at a lectern before thirty or so empty chairs, and "lectured" from my notes. Verbalizing what I had written down helped me to understand. Pretending that I had to explain the material to someone else clarified it for me. As you've discovered, a useful test of how well we do or don't understand something is to ask ourselves whether we can explain it successfully to others so that they can understand it.

Part of the joy of work, after all, is devising ways to achieve what needs to be done, putting them into effect, monitoring how well they're succeeding, and changing or sticking to an approach until the goal is met. One can achieve so much more than one thought possible through diligence, creative methods, flexible responses to changing conditions, and just plain doggedness.

All this should not suggest that I didn't enjoy my time at the university. Quite the contrary—I enjoyed it, in many ways, passionately; I was in a place I loved, spending my days immersed in great literature, and trying to earn the approval and respect of people I looked up to.

Why do so many people put themselves through the rigors of a formal education or professional training? Why did I? Why did you? Why do our students? The answers are many: some may say it's to prepare for a career, to get their money's worth, to fulfill their parents' expectations, to respond to peer pressure, or to prove something to themselves. But whether or not we realize it at the time, I believe that we do so to prepare ourselves to serve—with that "pastor's heart" I mentioned in another letter. A life in service to others is a life without regrets. "We serve our society best by keeping our integrity to whatever talent we have," says Nadine Gordimer. As I tell my students, what they are doing today with their time prepares them for people and experiences at other times and other venues in their lives.

If I had slacked off in high school, or if I had slipped and slid through my undergraduate years, or if I had applied myself half-heartedly to graduate studies—then I wouldn't now have the privilege of working with 160 new students every semester, nor would I have the privilege of writing to you, as I am, with whatever words of encouragement I can come up with. Although I didn't know it at the time, what I was learning in school was helping to prepare me for the students and friends (and, yes, correspondents) I would meet years later.

"But why must I study chemistry?" a student might ask. "I'll never do anything with it!" You study chemistry for the same reasons you study a myriad of seemingly unrelated courses and for the same reasons you accumulate and retain all kinds of knowledge and skills and experiences: to advance and broaden your thinking, to train your character, but most important, to prepare yourself for someone or something you'll encounter ten, perhaps twenty or thirty, years later. You prepare yourself to become more than what you are so that your life can be more than what it is, and more than you ever dreamed it could be. You do the work to *become*.

To some people, such single-mindedness might seem obsessive, but ask those devoted to their work, and they'll say the same thing: the most satisfying tasks require the utmost concentration. "There is no point in work," says D. H. Lawrence, "unless it absorbs you like an absorbing game"—an inner game, that is, where all serious daring begins. In his poem "SEXT" W. H. Auden agrees:

> You need not see what someone is doing
> to know if it is his vocation,
>
> you have only to watch his eyes:
> a cook mixing a sauce, a surgeon
>
> making a primary incision,
> a clerk completing a bill of lading,

> wearing the same rapt expression,
> forgetting themselves in a function.
>
> How beautiful it is,
> that eye-on-the-object look.

I credit my discipline in large part to the example set not only by my parents but also by my grandparents. In my mother's family, a love of work—with its stress on discipline and self-denial—was strong. Work was their play, and the blending of work and play was part of the ritual and rhythm of life. My mother's mother worked in her own way in the home with cooking, sewing, and cleaning and did a lot of church work until her physical frailties became limiting. My mother studied hard in school, rarely dating during the week. Even when her girlfriends called with invitations for socializing, she would decline because for her, homework was her priority. She remembers many nights sitting at the kitchen table until 1 a.m. pecking at the typewriter.

My mother also drew strength from the example of her father. One story that she tells draws the picture. Before she was born, he was a traveling salesman for New Home Sewing Machines. He was away a lot, and so when his new daughter was born, he announced, "By golly, I'm staying home with this kid." He found another sales job that enabled him to be with his family every night. "Speed-mo Stamp Pads Built Under High Pressure with Ink" was his slogan. By the time my mother was five or six, she often accompanied him on his route, sometimes sitting outside in the car to wait for him, other times going into the store with him. She could see from an early age how hard he worked, how he applied his intelligence, creativity, and diligence to getting the job done—sick or well. When he was at home, he worked in the small shop behind the house, where he made little metal boxes. It was precision work, beautifully crafted. Everything had to fit just right. Then he dipped them in enamel, baked them in an oven in the shop, and sold the finished pieces to his clients. When the Depression hit, he continued to make these and other metal crafts, but of course he didn't sell very many.

I can remember visiting my grandparents and standing in the

open doorway of the shop. "Grandpa, can I come in?" I would ask. "Oh no," he said. "You might get cut. Stay right by the door." So I would, watching as the heavy metal cutter crashed down onto the sheet metal, over and over. He'd answer my questions as he worked, or listened patiently to my schoolboy prattle, a faint smile on his lips as his hands remained in constant motion. To this day, the smell of enamel, cut steel, or metal filings brings to my mind those blissful weekends at the threshold of my grandpa's shop. His industriousness was a model not just for my mother but for my brother and me, too.

His attitude toward work rubbed off on my mother's sister as well, and from her I learned how important it is to keep on working regardless of age or physical challenges, remaining active in whatever field we choose, never giving up on our task or ourselves. If you were a professional, you worked, whatever else was going on, whatever else you felt about the rest of your life. My aunt served in the Women's Army Corps (1941–46), participated in the Manhattan Project at Los Alamos, and then relocated at the University of Chicago where she worked in metal analysis until 1973. In her seventies and still vigorous and eager to be working, my aunt decided that she would live this period as if her whole life were in front of her—good advice for all of us. Her voracious reading habits continued right to the end. She served as state representative for the American Association of Retired Persons (AARP). She made the most of each day. She, too, knew the importance of working hard, ignoring the clock, and always challenging herself. From her example I learned a lot about self-discipline.

Such was my heritage concerning the worth of work, and it has been a great gift; indeed, like you, I have learned from my family and my observation and my own experience that the opposite of work is not play but idleness. Being idle is utterly self-indulgent because we are not *investing* ourselves in anything, which leads to uselessly squandering time.

In his superb dramatic monologue *Ulysses*, Tennyson imagines the thoughts and feelings of the Homeric hero (along with some help from Dante's *Inferno*), who retired to private life at Ithaca. We find the bold adventurer idle, sitting with an aged wife by a quiet hearth, meting out laws to a savage race unable to understand their purpose. The old man recalls the exhilaration of his younger days: the heat of battle, the thrill of the journey, and the satisfaction of surmounting seemingly impossible obstacles. He hears the call of that intense activity and declares:

> I am a part of all that I have met;
> Yet all experience is an arch wherethrough
> Gleams that untravelled world, whose margin fades
> For ever and for ever when I move.

He decides to undertake the quest for that which gives meaning to his life once more, and to leave his son Telemachus the task of ruling his people. For Ulysses, stasis is a kind of living death. He must be fully engaged in and with life and the struggles it presents. His must be forever the indestructible life of an adventurer—"life piled on life"—and although he and his mariners are old, "Some work of noble note may yet be done." Until death overtakes him, his purpose now is the Victorian ideal:

> To sail beyond the sunset, and the baths
> Of all the western stars, until I die.

When I first encountered these lines, the poem had little to say to me. I was twenty-two and (like you) in the full bloom of life, and the word "retirement" just wasn't part of my personal lexicon. But now at fifty-seven as I'm writing this, I find myself embracing Ulysses' resolve and his final, justly famous crescendo: "To strive, to seek, to find, and not to yield." I call upon these words not to convince myself of the need for continued work—I've always loved dearly to work—but to help deflect the verbal blows of those who question my devotion to that ethic.

Tennyson wrote these lines in the period after the 1833 death of his close friend Arthur Henry Hallam, who would have become his brother-in-law had he lived. He said that writing the piece helped express his "feeling about the need of going forward, and braving the struggle of life." While critics justly praised the poem upon publication as uplifting, bracing the spirit to look to the future and keep cheerful in old age, some readers saw in it an old man abandoning his old wife, his responsibilities, and the people under his rule and leaving his son behind to get on with it. This is what W. H. Auden had in mind when he wrote, "What is *Ulysses* but a covert . . . refusal to be a responsible and useful person, a glorification of the heroic dandy?" It appeared to these readers that Tennyson's hero was "braving the struggle of life" by trying to escape it.

But if we read the poem as Tennyson intended it—as a metaphorical defense of the creative life—we will see and hear in it the refusal to accept societal definitions of age and retirement most eloquently expressed. Yes, it is a poem about escape, yet the escape is not from responsibility but from idleness and malaise. Nor is the poem about his wife or son. We don't even know what they said or thought or felt about Ulysses' impending departure. What we do know is that the poem is about someone, very much like you, Kelly, who possesses the one gift that makes the longest life seem short: a sense of purpose. To Ulysses, as indeed to us, to explore broadly and well was a sufficient task for a lifetime. Whatever misfortune came to him, there was never the dreaded ennui, the feeling of living mechanically from day to day that makes so many lives into little purgatories. By remaining true to his purpose, Ulysses can achieve his full potential, which is the greatest contribution we can make to our world and our fellow humans, as well as to ourselves.

If someone asks when I'm going to retire, my first response is, "From what?" When the pianist Roger Williams turned seventy-four, he told an interviewer, "I tell everyone that people retire to do the things they've always wanted to do, so I retired at three."

Barring ill health or mandatory termination, we retire only from that which we are tired of, bored with, spent on. We retire because we think it will make us happier or more comfortable. We retire because our work has become tedious. We retire because we are compelled by family circumstance or company pressures. But if we love our work, as so many do, then no matter how much we give to it, or how old we are, there's more to give, and to discover. Because we love our work, it's as if we do no work at all.

Not so long ago, sixty-five or seventy at the latest was the cutoff age for retirement. Now, in our profession, there's no such forced termination, and for many teachers, seventy (and older) is still an age of undiminished vigor. Like you, when I began teaching I was the youngest teacher on campus. Now I'm among the oldest, and most of the teachers who were here when I arrived have left. I've been in a unique position, straddling the fence between two generations—the newly minted Ph.D.'s and those closing in on their retirement years. It used to sadden me to see colleagues retire. How could they give all this up? The answer is that they couldn't, at least not entirely. Many have returned to teach part time; others are actively engaged in favorite research projects and traveling and taking courses themselves. They have confirmed the view that teaching is a profession we retire into and not out of.

How unjust it is to retire someone purely on the basis of chronological age. Competence has little to do with age, and yet we seem to have built this barrier that once you cross it, your work life is done. Think of the skill and knowledge that are lost. My paternal grandfather worked for forty years at a paper mill. Although perhaps to some his work may have seemed routine or trivial, in what he did he found a continual challenge and long-term satisfaction. And so when the manager of the firm said that perhaps my grandfather should be dismissed on the basis of his age, my father intervened immediately and wrote a letter in which he said: "One of the best things you can do for my father and our family is to keep him employed, because he doesn't have much to do outside of work and he'd prefer to stay on if you can keep him for a few years. Of course, if it reaches the point when he would not be able or would get hurt, let me know."

I've always admired my father for doing that. It would have been easy to acquiesce to social pressures that suggest an artificial and arbitrary connection between age and uselessness. The manager agreed to keep my grandfather on, and he worked for an additional four years, part time, making rounds at night to check the machinery and the locks on the door. He enjoyed this. When he turned seventy-three and the likelihood of personal injury on the job had grown, both my father and the manager agreed he should be let go.

"We'll take good care of him and his pension," said the manager. My grandfather took his leave quite well and lived another thirteen years. He never knew why he had stayed on beyond retirement age; he never knew about my father's intervention.

While work is meaningful in its own right in the things it helps us reveal to ourselves, it can give us much more. Concentrated work is also a way of shutting out at least for a while distracting or painful thoughts. I know of no better antidote for sorrow.

"Now comes the tough part—carrying on," said my friend as we drove to his home, mere hours after he had buried his twenty-one-year-old son, victim of a self-inflicted gunshot.

"I feel guilty I wasn't with him," Ron said. There had been no obvious warning. Distress over unemployment seemed to vanish after his son received a call offering a new position. Only later did his father learn that a half-hour before the shooting, his son's fiancée had called to say she wanted out of their relationship.

My friend's grief was palpable, an ache that came and went. Prayers and letters and friends helped a great deal, of course, but work is what kept him going. "It's the only time I don't think about what happened that night," he said. Ron was a jazz pianist who played twice a week at a Los Angeles hotel. A group of us often went there on Saturdays to hear him perform three sets. He had been playing the night that his son shot himself. We were with him when he received the call.

Grief buffeted him, but work kept him moving. While he was absorbed in his performance, the burden of remembering lifted, for awhile at least. It left him little time for brooding. Some who heard of my friend's almost obsessive need to keep working were shocked by what seemed to them like a father's heartlessness. Just the opposite. Ron was finding his way toward healing through his music; the simple act of "carrying on" was carrying him forward. He literally "worked" his way through his sorrow. Work was his salvation.

Kelly, I hope that your own work remains challenging and stimulating, and that it continues to lead you to as yet undiscovered places within yourself. I hope, too, that you'll find the opportunities to share with your students the inner peace and joy that come from working conscientiously, honestly, and wholeheartedly. Remind them that achievement matters and that what they do is less important than how they do it. Encourage them to do their best—and believe that they will. "The value of life lies, not in the length of days, but in the use we make of them," Montaigne reminds us. Indeed, the use we make of our allotted time makes us who we are.

I also hope that when the word *retirement* looms large over you that you'll be able to look back with pride of accomplishment, and not regret, knowing along with Thoreau that the worst thing in life is to reach the end and to know that we have not lived. Seize the moment, live fully—and advise your students to do the same.

And please continue to write to me—and to your other professors—about your progress. It's always good to hear from you.

Warm regards,

CHAPTER 14

When a Parent Dies

Dear Kelly,

I'm so sorry to hear about the death of your father. I hope it doesn't sound presumptuous to say that I felt as though I knew him myself, based on all the kind words you said about him and the anecdotes you told in our conversations and letters. My thoughts and prayers go out to you and your family that you will be comforted during this difficult time.

Although inevitable and sometimes even a blessing when it brings suffering to an end, the death of anyone close is always a severe loss. Yes, your father lived eighty-four years, and yes, that is a long life, but it never seems to have been long enough when death takes from us our loved ones, especially our parents. Your bond with him is unlike any other. In many significant ways you were and are closer to him than you'll ever be to your friends or siblings or future husband. He knew you better than could anyone else except your mother, who knows you in still different ways. He was there from the beginning. He is a part of you. How fortunate you were to have grown up in a loving home, in an atmosphere of confidence and harmony, surrounded by people who had a sound sense of what is worthwhile, who didn't just talk about the moral and religious life, but practiced it. Along with those memories, your father has left you with the immeasurable gift of a story to tell—and someday, when you've absorbed and made peace with his death, you'll begin to write it.

After my own father died in 2005, my brother and I received many letters of consolation. One of the most meaningful came from a dear colleague whose words may now help you as well:

No one wants to say good-bye to a father whose scope and breadth encompassed the entire horizon. Dale, even as you grieve, you will begin to bring your father to life for all of us as you set yourself to the task of telling his story. He will be your companion as you write, your companion as you read, and your companion at every book signing. He will be free now to be wherever he chooses, and he will choose to be with you. And rightly so, for you have been the ideal son, the son every father wishes for, the son your father received. May you be at peace knowing peace is the gift you gave your father.

No doubt, peace seems a long way off from you right now, but that will change. C. S. Lewis has written, "Some great good comes from the dead to the living in the months or weeks after the death, as if Our Lord welcomed the newly dead with the gift of some power to bless those they have left behind." I believe that. The day after my father's funeral I returned to campus to teach my Shakespeare class for which, coincidentally, I had assigned *Hamlet* two weeks before. As I opened the discussion, I saw my father, seated at the back of the room and dressed in the dark blue suit, light blue shirt, and red tie he had worn for his fiftieth wedding anniversary and, now, eleven years later, he was buried in. He was listening intently, as he always did when either of his sons spoke. When I recited Hamlet's words— "As long as I have memory, as long as I live, I will remember you, and what you have told me"—I was speaking to my father. When I talked about Hamlet's broodings on death and the life hereafter and then said the lines, "There's a divinity that shapes our ends, / Rough-hew them how we will," my father was taking in every word. And when I concluded the hour, he gave me his familiar nod of approval as if to say: "You did well. Stay with it." Afterward one student remarked that he had never heard the play discussed with such passion or belief. There is some of Hamlet in us all because there is some of our father in us all.

In the days that followed, Dad seemed very near to me, and that, too, comforted me. This feeling is akin to one I had many years ago when he accompanied me to my campus to meet with the president of my college. As we stepped out of the car and approached the administration building, with my father on my right wearing his dark blue suit and red tie, suddenly I felt a wave of strength coming from him. Afterward I asked him about it, and he explained that it was his way of buoying himself up for the meeting. "I just thought about some of the things I'd done in life," he said, and it was that solidarity I had sensed. I still do. Thus his spirit has remained a vibrant presence in my life, and so, Kelly, will your father's in yours.

You told me of the circumstances of your dad's passing, and I was reminded of my own experience. Dad died on October 2. My wife lovingly cared for him and spoke to him through the day before (for which I'll always be grateful), and then I took over that evening until 11 p.m. When I left him he was asleep, breathing easily. At 7:35 the next morning the call came and the nurse gently said, "Dale, I'm very sorry but we lost your father."

I told my son, who said, "I'm going with you."

I called my wife on her cell phone, but before I could speak more than her name she said, "What time did he die?"

I went upstairs to find my mother sitting on the edge of her bed, still wearing her nightgown, fidgeting with her hearing aids. I wrote on a pad the words: "We've lost Dad. He stopped breathing this morning at 7:30. He was comfortable and asleep. Ryan is going with me to see him. Patti will stay with you."

With a deep breath, Mom took in the news. I gave her a hug. "Are you okay?" I asked her. She nodded. I could feel her sadness and also her relief.

My son and I drove the twenty minutes to the rehab center where my father had been cared for since breaking his hip six months earlier. Ryan waited outside the room as I entered. Dad was lying on his bed, as if asleep, blanket up to his chest, mouth open. All the equipment had been removed. The curtains were pulled aside, the window was open, there was a soft, caressing breeze. The sun beamed down "like a benediction," Mark Twain wrote, a line that seemed appropriate as I stood there, at that moment viewing, for the first time, my father in death, not in life. I invited Ryan in and reminded him of a story he had read in ninth grade titled "Shaving," about a son caring for his ailing father. I shaved off my father's three-days' growth of whiskers and clipped a hangnail from his left little finger.

"I'm going to miss him," Ryan said.

Many times during my father's final months I just wanted to wrap

my arms around him and protect him, like a child. Now I didn't
need to. He was safe, and I carried no worries—only peace and calm
and a sense of the rightness of this event, despite the loss it inevitably
entailed.

The night before the funeral my family, my brother, and I were
able to sit for four hours alone with the open casket, and it was a very
important time for us—a lovingly peaceful time. Lying there, my
father looked sixty, not eighty-four, with a senator's dignity, confidence, strength. At one point I slipped into his inner coat pocket an
envelope containing a two-page handwritten letter to him that I had
composed that morning. We all found our own ways to say goodbye,
and it's important that you find yours.

Sometimes when people feel overwhelmed by their loss, Kelly,
it helps to remind themselves that in Beethoven's *Eroica Symphony*,
the funeral march we all so readily identify with sadness comes in
the second movement and not in the last; death is not the end. Certainly my father understood this heart-deep, as I was to discover in
a special way the day after he died. I was searching in his files for
his mother's maiden name and came across a folder marked "MA's
funeral." Inside I found a carbon copy of a two-page letter he had
sent in 1982 to his brothers after their mother's death:

> Wouldn't it be terrible if we buried our loved ones and that was the
> end? What would life be without the great cloud of witnesses of those
> who have passed on but are with us as our eternal cheering section? I
> am at peace because I believe in the Resurrection. Without it, there is
> nothing—no forgiveness, no desire for growth, no hereafter. When I
> stood beside the bed of MA, I knew this would not be the end of it.
> . . . This life is only a small part of the whole of eternity. We have a lot
> of friends who have passed away. They are with us.

This was my father's way of speaking to me from beyond, and
I knew in an instant that I had to read it at the funeral the next
day. The forty-five-minute service was held in the early afternoon
with full military honors. (My father had been a naval man, having
served in the Pacific, for which he received a nomination for a Silver
Star and retired as a commander.) The service was conducted qui-

etly and with dignity. My father never liked a lot of fanfare. When I read the excerpt from his letter, I felt him speaking through me.

Along with the pleasant pressures of my academic work, what helped me through this period was my father's practical philosophy about death. Over the years I had watched him conduct himself with great strength and seeming ease after his own father and then youngest brother and then mother and then another brother died. I had helped him to prepare a folder marked "When that time comes" that contained everything my brother and I would need to know to carry us through the preparations, the funeral, the burial, and the events after. With him I had visited the spot that he and my mother had selected for their final resting place. A photograph shows him pointing up to the crypt. During the last ten years of his life, as my brother and I, and our mother especially, cared for him during his battles first with rheumatoid arthritis, then cancer, then kidney failure, then the broken hip, and finally pneumonia—not once did I hear from him a complaint against God because, as he said often with bracing honesty and no self-pity, he could never repay God the favors He had done him.

What has also helped me is the knowledge that we did all that we could do for him. Once when I arrived at the facility and greeted him in his wheelchair outside his room, and again when he was enfeebled and in intensive care, my father looked at me, took my right hand, raised it to his lips, and gently kissed it. Later I asked my mother what Dad meant. "Oh, many things, Dale," she said. "How proud he was of you and Glenn. How much he loved you. How grateful he was for all you'd done. And so much more." My father had completed his work, as my wife had told him in her special way the day before he died, and he was ready to go.

All of us grieve differently, Kelly, and you and your family will find your own way. Like my father, my mother is a very private person, self-reliant and independent. In the days after the funeral, we wanted to be quietly alone together and with our thoughts. Invitations to go to dinner, to socialize, were offered with the kindest intentions, but we didn't feel a need to orchestrate good times to block out sad thoughts. My mother's rock-solid faith, her strength, and the clarity and insight that have developed from a lifetime of reading would sustain her through the weeks and months ahead. So, too, would her certainty that she would see her husband again. "We'll get through this," she said to me after the funeral, and she was right.

Nevertheless, some observers may judge your reactions. Ignore them. One person, blinded by his own definition of what it means to be human and how one should deal with loss, couldn't understand why my mother during those first days and weeks preferred quiet over noise, tranquility over activity, solitude over constant company. Another, a neighbor, revealed her attitudes toward grieving when she tried to pressure me into moving my mother into a facility where, as she put it, "she'll be among others." I kept my composure and only said, "I know my mother very well." When I told my mother, she was vehement. "Isn't that terrible," she said. "Why do people say such things?" She marched right across to the neighbor's house and assured her that she was quite content where she was.

"People don't understand if you don't do things their way," Mom said to me later. "We're all so different and our lives are so different, the way we've been brought up. You've got to let people live as they want to." My mother wanted to continue to do things at her pace. "I want to play the piano when I feel like it, read when I feel like it, work on my book about Beethoven when I feel like it." What the neighbor had failed to accept was that my mother—before or after my dad's death—couldn't stand having people (other than family members) around her all the time. "They'd drive me crazy," she said.

What I'm trying to say here is that well- or ill-intentioned people may try to intervene in your struggle with your grief, but in the end, the process of dealing with death is ultimately your own. You aren't obligated to explain what you do, or how, or when. If you feel that an action or preference or behavior will honor both your father and the validity of your feelings of love *and* loss, then follow your heart. People either will understand, or, sadly for them, they won't.

At times, Kelly, you'll feel fear. It will sneak up on you, suddenly and unannounced, and you'll know that it is an expression of your grief, and a necessary stage of letting go. At these times, be alone and observant. Acknowledge the fear. Slowly it will open up to you—and you'll see the reason for it. Give thanks for your father's life—and, I promise you, the fear will evaporate, and with time you'll be changed because something new has entered your heart.

No doubt you've also discovered the heartache that comes from the absence of his voice. Missing now are the recorded messages on my answering machine (typically, "Dale . . . Dad. Give me a call when you have a moment"). Or the arrival in the mail of a newspaper clipping or magazine article he thought I'd like to read. Missing, too, are the opportunities to call him, as I did almost daily, when I had a question or to tell him of something I saw or read that I wanted to share with him. Most of all, absent are the words of encouragement and support that he was so good at imparting whenever I needed them. His words, "How's the work going?" were an entry into a place where our ideas and feelings and knowledge could meet and mingle. Now that door is closed.

We were fortunate. We had six months to say goodbye. Not all have that opportunity. Over the months, too, Mom had learned what it was to live alone without him. One day, two weeks before he died, I was able to bring him home for four hours. The day was epiphany-filled. Remember, Kelly, my father had been away from his home for more than five months—and yet during that day he emerged from his confusion and embraced everything he saw. I took three pages of verbatim notes of what he said, his almost continual expressions of wonder and amazement. He even was able to sit at the dining room table for a meal with us—a last supper as it were—and the next day when he awoke back at the center, the nurse said there was a smile on his face.

"What do you feel?" she asked.

"Optimism and goodwill," he said.

Without my father's gentle but consistent prodding and entire devotion, neither my brother nor I would be where we are today in our respective careers and personal lives. He has been at the heart of everything I've done, everything I've been, and everything I hope to be. And that is why I continue to be so ambitious, so driven. And why so much of what I have done in my life has been in the hope of evoking his pride. It is to be worthy. It is to honor him.

No day goes by in which he doesn't enter my mind. Your father will remain in yours, too.

Mom and I visited the crypt site the weekend after the service. It was cool, quiet, and reassuring, just the way he would have wanted it. May you find that kind of peace.

Warm regards,

CHAPTER 15

Intimations of Mortality

Dear Kelly,

Set aside all distractions. Be still, listen, and soon you might connect deep inside with a universal whisper, or a constant whirring, or perhaps an ache that grows or even rages. It comes from a fact we are all subconsciously aware of every moment of our life: Time is fleeting, and one day each of us must die. If you truly listen, you may even hear yourself ask, "Am I using my allotted time well?" Many of us feel these intimations as we pass landmark birthdays in middle age, while others become conscious of them as early as childhood.

Ever since you told me of your father's death, I've been thinking about mortality and the meaning and importance of art and work in light of humanity's common, ultimate fate. It seems to me that a fundamental lie about life prevails in our society: we think it will last forever, and we deny the inevitable fact that one day it will end. Few people talk about death, read about it, or think about it. Instead, so many of our frenetic activities seem to be ratcheted up to fever pitch in order to shield us from the reality of eventual decline and demise. Many individuals sleepwalk through life, pretending that it will go on forever or, at least, ignoring the fact that it won't. In our era there are a great many who seem apathetic, unfeeling with a vengeance, as if by downplaying the preciousness of life they can avoid the pain of its end.

We can hear this apathy in the erosion of the language of emotion and the blurring of the reality of death. Great joy or good fortune or wonder or dreams fulfilled or miracles occurring elicit the common observation that "It was great!" or "Wow!" The birth of a child and an ice cream flavor are reduced to emotional equivalence by the same, increasingly meaningless, descriptor: "awesome." On the other hand, serious, life-changing events are trivialized. A witness tells a television interviewer that a drive-by shooting victim was "whacked" or "wasted" or "blown away." Horrifying auto accidents or devastating fires are termed "spectacular." Murder victims are merely "bodies" that are "dumped" (like so much garbage) along a roadside. Graphic images of maimed, bleeding children in war-torn nations are just "casualties," and soldiers tragically sacrificed by their own peers in the confusion of battle are "victims of friendly fire." One might never suspect that such phrases are describing the death of a human being.

The development of attitudes that minimize the magnitude of death stems from many sources. Certainly, persuasive strategies used by advertisers, corporations, and governments emphasize the manipulation of language and meaning for the purpose of controlling behaviors and choices. Platitudes and banality often rule in messages emanating from our mass-mediated, wired, digital culture. For example, Madison Avenue is hell-bent on perpetuating the Myth of Eternal Youth, as if applying the right face cream, eating the right breakfast cereal, or taking the latest "wellness" medication can somehow build a wall between us and the irrevocable conclusion to every human's story. These messages don't merely denigrate death's importance; they encourage us to deny its existence.

Yet mortality is a subject highly worthy of sustained and intense concentration, and to talk about this openly and honestly through the subjects we teach helps to lift students from present concerns. Such explorations must be undertaken with caution, however. In every classroom at least one student will have recently experienced a tragic loss of some kind. In time, Kelly, you'll be able to discern how far to push with this topic, or how quickly to withdraw.

There are many ways to get our students to consider the realities about death and to see it as a component of our lives. Reading great books is one, for one of the things they can do for us—besides offering pleasure—is to show us the commonalities of the human condition. We can't plunge into Hans Christian Andersen or the great melodramatist Charles Dickens, for example, without learning about peoples' many frailties and uncertainties. Almost every writer of consequence—from Aeschylus to Walker Percy to Philip Roth—has had something to say about the subject. "*All* writing of the narrative kind, and perhaps all writing," says Margaret Atwood, "is motivated, deep down, by a fear of and a fascination with mortality—by a desire to make the risky trip to the Underworld, and to bring something or someone back from the dead."

All sorrows have virtually the same source. When I was nineteen, a professor asked us to create a narrative in which we imagined what we would do with only one year left to live. Then she encouraged us to compose our own four-hundred-word obituary. Suddenly, we had to remove ourselves from peripheral concerns to consider what is most essential in life. By meditating on our end, we were encouraged to make a new beginning, to focus again or perhaps for the first time on the inherent value of each hour, each day.

One of my graduate study partners—a Jesuit priest then earning his doctorate in English literature—gave me a brilliantly imaginative exercise that I sometimes share with my students. Consider yourself now at your end, stretched upon your bed, weary and in pain and alone—expecting at any moment to slip away. Your hair has turned white, your skin is dry and wrinkled, and your eyes have grown dim. Consider the hour of death not as something in the far-distant future, but as if it is now present. Consider what would most trouble you at that hour. Follow the voyage of your body. Consider its dissolution in the grave. And most important to this priest and his faith, follow the journey of your soul.

What do you feel? Fear or horror at the prospect? Or a calm, mild acceptance of the inevitable? With time, and experience, and courage, you'll find yourself shearing away all cant and nonessential elements of your personality and looking with humor on the follies of the world—from the position of an objective observer. You'll see how little you have understood what life is really for. You'll see what you have thrown away. Over time, this can go beyond a single weekly exercise.

Another way to help your students see death at a deeper level is to lead them through a philosophical thought experiment. Ask them to consider this fact: in one hundred years, all 6.5 billion people on

Earth now will be gone—and replaced by an entirely new cast and crew. Encourage your students to really try to grapple with the implications of this. How might this bigger picture reorient their view of many of the mundane issues with which they concern themselves? Seeing the vastness and universality of mortality can inspire them to embrace with all their fervency the fact that they are alive here and now. "Thinking about death," Albert Schweitzer says, "produces life."

A fourth way to open their minds to the topic is to tell stories from your own experience. When I was in junior high school, for example, I became convinced that I had a terminal illness. The story of my growing fear, its resolution, and what I learned about myself and my relationship to my parents has proved to be for me a powerful way to introduce a poem or a novel or a play that has at its center the subject of mortality.

Saturday morning stretched before me, lazy and idyllic. I was thirteen years old, had completed seventh grade, and was looking forward to ten carefree weeks of summer vacation. I showered and dried myself, and as I bent over I noticed two tiny but ominous-looking pairs of jagged white lines on each shoulder. No discomfort, no pain: they were just there, as if someone had taken a dull knife and drawn it against my skin, leaving a light welt in its wake. A quick stab of worry shot through me.

We've all heard stories of medical students who, while studying a particular specialty—cardiology, for example—begin to see in themselves the signs of the very illness they are investigating. It took my father enormous willpower to resist self-diagnosis during a year-long course in abnormal psychology. Every problem became a mirror in which he was tempted to see reflected some fault in himself.

Could this explain my symptoms? I thought over the biology I had studied in my classes, but the marks resembled nothing, even remotely, that I had studied. Nor did any of the science books that I consulted in my father's library offer an answer, although there were disquieting, if vague, similarities in some of the photographs of tumors and other growths.

Imagination can motivate and focus our reason as no other power, or it can be one of the deepest sources of error with which we must contend. "Put the world's greatest philosopher on a plank that is wider than need be," Pascal says; "if there is a precipice below, although his reason may convince him that he is safe, his imagination will prevail." And so during the next two months my adolescent imagination encouraged me to leap from concern to suspicion to conviction that what I had was an early indication of cancer. In those days, and in my limited experience, cancer was a death sentence, and as I imagined the worst, I realized that I was far from being prepared to die. Instead, I was terrified, and my fear made me feel deflated and uncertain. It seems that the solid rock of my future, even my present, had been jolted to pieces.

Each time I tried to tell my parents, however, I couldn't get the words out. Why? Because I was afraid of being ridiculed? No, for buried deep in me were their consoling words, "Dale, remember: You can come to us about anything." Was I afraid of hearing the worst? Yes, but also I knew that to admit my fear was to admit my weakness. Pride stood in the way.

And so instead of appropriating all that I had learned—I waited, and waited, hoping (wishing) the marks would disappear. Like many people, too, I tried to divert my mind from troubling thoughts by turning to new concerns. I pretended the marks weren't there. I kept busy. Although I sought to repress my fear, it wouldn't go away. Its approach was steady, unrelenting.

I can't remember what led to my decision to let go. All I recall is that the inner pressure was too great. I realized, finally, that I couldn't alter the past; I couldn't predict the future. Only the present moment was in my power.

One evening after dinner, in the privacy of my bedroom with the door shut and as tears prickled at my eyelids, I sat on the edge of my bed and showed my father the marks on my shoulders. He bent down and looked closely under the illumination of a desk lamp. If he, too, was alarmed, he didn't reveal it. Like my mother—steady, thoughtful, wise—he wasn't given to emotional extremes.

"I'm sure it's nothing," he said as he stood up, "but if it'll make you feel better I'll make an appointment with Dr. Klatch." His tone was casual, as if he had announced: "Well, it's a warm summer day. Let's go for a walk."

I have strong memories of our drive to the doctor's office: the fluttering in my stomach, the restlessness I felt as a child whenever I faced the unknown. I stared straight ahead all the way, having nothing to say. And I remember Dr. Klatch: a nearly bald, dapper man with a wry sense of humor. Before he even examined me, he surprised me by asking questions about my feelings, my thoughts. Then fifteen minutes later and only after I had said all I wanted to say, did he examine me. He took one look and with a happy smile he said something like: "Well, you don't need to worry. They're called stria—stretch marks. This is all a natural stage of growing up. Eventually they may fade away."

It was an exceptionally warm and bright summer day that somehow I had failed to notice when I rode to the doctor's office, but now, on leaving, the vitality came at me with such an intensity that I couldn't take it all in. The greens and blues and pinks fairly cried out in their fervor. The air smelled fresh. I was bombarded by a piercing beauty. And a thrill of gladness ran through me.

Philosophers tell us that a sudden personal awareness of life's ephemeral nature often produces deep and full love. After the death of his sister, Abraham Maslow wrote, "I am stabbed by the beauty of flowers and babies." Mary Pipher told of a "tremendous sweetness" in the evanescent. At thirty-one, four years before his own death, Mozart wrote to his father: "Since death is the true end purpose of our life, I have made it my business . . . to get to know this true, this best friend of man so well that the thought of him not only holds no terrors for me but even brings me the good fortune and opportunity to get to know death as the key to our true happiness." Sociologists call these times *liminal moments*—when a door opens wide to personal transformation.

Now as I look back on my experience and think of people I've known who have *really* faced imminent death, my adolescent fear strikes me as rather absurd; and yet because of it I became a different kind of person. I was still Dale, but now Dale more grown up: awake, clear, relaxed, intensely alive—and thankful.

But how easy it is for me or for anyone to write about the subject of death from the safe distance of a reader or observer. With what carefree abandon we as children played cowboys and Indians, or sat before a shoot-out in a movie, knowing that the actor had not really died. Until the reality of death strikes us personally, none of us knows it truly. Then and only then, when we are at our most vulnerable, do our lives powerfully change. Leo Tolstoy, himself a death-watcher, understood this very well.

You will recall from your reading of his bleakly honest but humane novella *The Death of Ivan Ilych* that the protagonist (like so many of us at one time or another) is by nature a proud creature, self-reliant, prone to depend on his abilities, background, education, and resourcefulness to sustain him. He allows himself the illusion that he has control over his fate, even to the point of pushing death away to some distant, unnamed, even unacknowledged necessity that's "out there." But as he learns during the course of the novella, there is always, lurking at the boundaries of life, this limitation from which even he cannot escape.

And as Ivan comes to realize, the only way out of fear is through it, and only God can get him there. The hour of his greatest hope is when at a moment of deep regret he thinks, "He whose understanding mattered would understand." When he can no longer rely upon himself or the doctors or family for answers, when he gives up the charade that he is independently powerful, then he is strengthened, empowered. We cannot make these mortal bodies last indefinitely, Tolstoy seems to be saying; no matter how careful or caring we are, our physical aspect will at some point cease to exist.

When she was twenty-three, one of my colleagues attended a Van Cliburn piano concert with her child and husband. Suddenly she realized a day would come when she would die, but Cliburn's music would go on—and she cried. This was the first time she considered her mortality heart-deep.

Why are our hearts troubled at such times? Gerard Manley Hopkins's poem "Spring and Fall" helps us here. A little girl named Margaret weeps over the golden leaves of the autumn forest, all fallen to the ground, but doesn't know why. The older, more experienced narrator, who knows what she does not, tells her that someday she, too, will understand: "It is the blight man was born for, / It is Margaret you mourn for." None of us wants to die, but can you imagine seeing a pregnant woman and saying to her, "keep the child from coming out into life, for that will inevitably lead to death"? No, this life of encounters is so far better than the life of safety in the womb.

Tolstoy's novella, like all memento mori, opens our eyes to the truth by telling us of many reasons we avoid grappling with death's effect on our lives. Like Ivan Ilych, if we think about our end, we are forced to evaluate the worth of how we are living; and if we have made poor use of our years, we fear the guilt and regret that might accompany our death. (Remember his words: "What if my whole life has really been wrong?") Or we fear not so much the prospect of death but what may lead up to it—dependence, loss of dignity, mental deterioration, pain. (It's the intractable pain that makes Ivan feel so alone.) Some people may fear what they believe to be an entry into nonbeing, the dread of insignificance, the unmitigating blankness of death, bereft of spiritual deliverance. The dreadful prospect of forgetting, or being unheard of and unnoticed in an indifferent universe, is another reason Ivan pushes thoughts of death away: I will cease to exist; there will be nothing—and yet the world will go on, the sun will continue to rise, the wind will blow, and people will go on without me. Perhaps the greatest fear for some people arises from the religious conviction that the fact of dying is inseparable from the act of divine judgment, and many tremble to think what that verdict will be. Compared with this fear, the physical pain of dying is nothing.

But I suspect that none of these explanations applies to you, Kelly, as much as something else. You may be trying to reconcile the truth about mortality with your strong desire to complete your good and useful work. You've devoted a third of your life to bring you to this point, with a rich future ahead. You know your purpose, and when one knows it as clearly as you do, there is little patience for the distractions that come from people who do not know theirs, or will not concede that their time to find and perform good work, whatever form it takes, is necessarily limited. This understanding urges you on with your own work. Don't delay. Time is in short supply, that inner voice seems to be saying. *Carpe diem.*

"Blessed is the man [or woman]," says Thomas à Kempis, "who keeps the hour of his death always in mind, and daily prepares himself to die." As teachers we are called, I believe, to celebrate life, and in part we do this by taking an honest, unblinking look at our own mortality and that of our students.

Warm regards,

CHAPTER 16

A Sad Art

Dear Kelly,

"Teaching is a sad art."

I imagine you are as surprised to read these words as I was to hear them from Jacques Barzun thirty-five years ago. After all, haven't my letters emphasized the positive aspects of our chosen profession? Haven't I celebrated the many ways that colleagues and students enrich our minds, our experience, our very being? Isn't the most compelling aspect of our professional lives the fact that we are paid to do the work we love? What is so sad about any of that?

Well, to use the word in this context is not an invitation to despair. I'm not implying, as some might, that over the years our profession loses any of its luster or charm or sparkle, or that our work in and out of the classroom necessarily leads to burnout and depression. Nor am I connecting *sad* with the gravity of some subjects we teach or the bleakness of some books or the failure of some students.

No, it goes deeper than any of that.

As a child living in Amherst, Massachusetts, I grew up hearing the poetry of Robert Frost. "Birches," "Apple-picking," "Stopping by Woods on a Snowy Evening," among others, spoke truthfully to me of a world that I knew and of a people that I was raised among.

On occasion, Mr. Frost would visit the college, and so my father, an administrator at the nearby university, invited me one evening to a fireside chat arranged for a select number of students and faculty. In my mind's eye I see myself as a ten-year-old sitting cross-legged in my bathrobe, pajamas, and slippers. The expression on my face is bemused. In the background sits the poet, with his big white head and hanging brows, smiling boyishly as he gazes at his audience.

I remember none of his spoken words, of course, but I do re-member his tone and the feeling it left with me. Here was a good-humored, soft-spoken, larger-than-life figure in whom I sensed a peculiar sadness—a sadness, as I learned much later, that in an odd paradox grew more pronounced the more blessed he felt.

"Nothing gold can stay," says Frost in a poem by the same name, a reality he faced every day in his work as indeed we must face in ours. To step into the classroom and connect meaningfully with the students (as Frost himself did for many years) is to suffer some ache of separation when the term is over. To experience breakthroughs in the laboratory and advance in our field of inquiry is to lament the day when someone takes over and carries our work farther than we ever could have. To attach our devotion to any classic of literature or music or art is to invite a kind of inevitable humiliation, for the clas-sic itself will far outlive both ourselves and our inadequate attempts to understand and appreciate it. Like Frost, who knew so well the short-lived satisfaction of the creative instinct, we discover how quickly the seasons appear to pass if we are immersed in what we love to do. When we find our true vocation, when we have learned to recognize a compelling purpose to teach, then we don't want its challenges and considerable satisfaction to end.

In part, this feeling is related of course to the passage of time—of which there is never enough for reading all the books or writing all the essays or teaching all the classes we would like. We grow older, but our students seem not to, and each year we see the image of our younger selves reflected in the faces of eighteen- and nineteen- and twenty-year-olds; and mixed with our delight in the work is a nos-talgia for when we were in school—a less complicated, relatively free time, our lives filled with as yet untapped potential. The classroom becomes a kind of memento mori, therefore, and Wordsworth's "still, sad music of humanity" becomes our music, subtle yet insistent, as one year blends into another, and we indulge in the sensations of every possible moment lest that be the final opportunity to do so. And at commencement, as we watch the students walk by with their diplomas, we realize that most of these good people we'll never see again. Most of them were not yet alive when we were born, but a more poignant truth is that they will likely be here long after we are gone.

As you progress in your career, Kelly, it's important that you remain vigilant (as did Frost all his life) for any telltale signs of a dwindling of your own youthful fire. When William Dean Howells, filled with regret that his best years were gone, was about to leave Paris to care for his dying father in the United States, he said something to his friend Jonathan Sturges that ought to be emblazoned upon the office wall of every teacher: "Oh, you are young, you are young—be glad of it: be glad of it and live. Live all you can: it's a mistake not to. . . . I haven't done so—and now I'm old. It's too late. It has gone past me—I've lost it. You have time. You are young. Live!"

Example is probably better than explanation at this point. I discovered the above passage bracketed in one of my professor's texts. Soon after he had died at age seventy-seven, his son invited me to peruse his library of more than nine thousand books for some I might like to have. In volume after volume the penciled marginalia, all in his own hand, testified to an unquenchable vitality, to a mind deeply engaged in what he was reading at the time, to a man fully alive to the text and, by implication, to the world. I remembered that same vitality and good sense infusing his classroom as he raced along and we tried to keep up with our notes. It was a privilege just to watch this wonderfully learned man at work and leading the sort of life I was hoping to lead someday. Each day I came away feeling my *self* enlarged, alert, and refreshed.

I had every reason, therefore, to assume of my professor that with age and experience came confidence and personal security. But as the son revealed to me that afternoon at his home, behind his father's moral earnestness and vibrant spirit an ominous sense of unease had been working away toward the end of his professional life. Some mornings he awoke, sweating with fear that whatever had made him able to work the day before had vanished, and that he would go to his classroom and find himself paralyzed. Or he would toss and turn at night, wondering whether he had perpetuated through his lectures as much misunderstanding as understanding, as much error as truth. Students reported that his lectures became less sonorous, more jagged, more on edge; photos from the time show that his face had grown wax-pale and drained. Consumed with self-doubt and a conviction that something dreadful but indefinable had gone wrong, he developed an impregnable carapace around his inner self, refusing to share his deep personal feelings and thoughts with his wife or close friends. "I don't know why," his son told me, "but he went stale and lost interest in everything—and as he sank, I saw the effects of that on him, and on Mom, and on his students."

This sense of almost intolerable strain is familiar to innumerable creative people—not just teachers—reminding me of what Thoreau wrote a century and a half ago: "The mass of men lead lives of quiet desperation." In my many years as a college professor, I've witnessed or heard of three nervous breakdowns, one suicide, and seven firings, as well as numerous infidelities, habitual backbiting, and a handful of student-filed grievances for alleged sexual harassment, or worse. And each time, I've wondered (naïvely, I now realize) how and why so many maladies could bedevil such a seemingly noble, stimulating profession that offers so much to its practitioners, its students, its community, and the world at large.

Teaching (like writing) is not a job—it is a state of mind with a unique set of assumptions. One commentator has likened the teacher's life to one long, arduous journey of self-analysis—sometimes painful, sometimes "joyous, victorious and beautiful"—that requires not only a stripping away of our illusions, poses, and pretenses of all kinds but also both the vision to see beyond our faults, no matter how dismaying, and the tenacity to keep working toward our potential through all manner of discouragements. Perhaps it is this inherent challenge that first attracts many of us to the profession.

Periods of anxiety and dissatisfaction are not uncommon even among seasoned teachers. You say that you feel neither as well-read nor as confident and mature as you had hoped? Your mastery of a particular novel is somewhat unsure? Your grasp of a literary genre is not without contradictions? I'm not surprised. I would be much more concerned if a caring, competent teacher like yourself didn't go through such periods, for the alternatives are overblown self-confidence or callous indifference. Don't imagine teaching is easy, and don't give up when you find that it's hard. "Tussle with the difficult things," says Robertson Davies, "and in the end they will reveal their meaning to you, and that meaning may help you over many a difficult place." Even for the most accomplished men and women, it is never easy bridging the gap between where we are and where we want to be, between what we are and what we would like to become. As an undergraduate, the distance between the lectern of my English literature professor and the front row of desks where I sat was a mere eight feet, but I knew instinctively that it would take many years and much effort to cross that divide and earn the inestimable privilege of standing where he then stood.

But as Frost knew well as both a writer and a teacher, so we, too, learn: art extorts a high price from its creators. If he were here today, Kelly, he'd say to you or to any ambitious creative artist—write all the books you care to write, teach all the classes you want to teach, give of yourself to your students and to your institution, but try not to let your busy professional life irreparably skew your sense of proportion and balance. There's a lot to lose if we fail to fulfill our dreams of professional success, but even more to lose if in pursuing those dreams we end up neglecting the one person who is, beyond all others, our deepest concern: our innermost self. "It is the fundamental, animating element in your intellectual and emotional life," says Robertson Davies, "and you must be very careful of it."

What the son of my professor believed overwhelmed his father can entrap any of us, if we ignore the self: without our realizing it, intellectual and spiritual torpor, indifference, and lethargy can take root; our sensibilities wither; our relationships with people, including students, become stunted; and we end up emotionally shriveled, no longer able to draw sustenance from the life we've chosen. A chronic lack of enthusiasm, a refusal to take risks, a lost capacity to feel—all these are symptoms of this phenomenon. Or my professor could have been depressed, perhaps not because he ignored the self or was bored or apathetic, as his son implied, but because of chemical changes in the body and the aging process and a lifetime of griefs. In any event, Frost himself battled this every day, and to some extent so must we.

But this is not the only potential for sadness inherent in teaching. In Jacques Barzun's analysis of the profession, he says that "the regard for it is a lost tradition." Indeed, there is no shortage of critics waiting to embrace our discomforts. Few understand the courage it takes to step into a classroom. Complain to the general public and you'll witness a dozen "knowing" nods among those who harbor contempt for the hard work of achieving academic mastery.

If ever you feel you're not taken seriously by society, and if that pains you, don't let the critical voices embitter or discourage you. We live in a society in which there is at most only a partial comprehension of that slow, deliberate, exhaustive search for truth that is the quest of every serious student and teacher and writer. We live in a culture that tends to denigrate reason and applaud feeling. Many individuals outside the profession neither understand nor appreciate the energy, expertise, and effort that go into making the classroom a crucible of ideas and learning. No matter what blind spots the surrounding culture suffers from, teach the best you can in the circumstances in which you find yourself. Wealth, status, or power are not the only standards by which quality of life is measured. Be careful not to let such ignorance of or apathy about the nature of your work awaken in you any spite. You do not teach to earn the world's approval or support; if you adopt that attitude, the inevitable disappointment will grate upon you, honing a hardened edge, and you'll compromise the reasons you're in the classroom to begin with: a love of learning, a respect for students, and a desire to master your field. To paraphrase Aldous Huxley, experience is not what happens to us; it is what we do with what happens to us.

Kelly, please don't confuse my cautionary observations with negativity or pessimism about our work. My purpose here (as in all of my letters) is not to undermine teaching but to uncover as much about the profession as I possibly can, and that includes explaining some of its inherent perils. Idealism by itself can be a fragile foundation; tempered with an honest, open realism, it can foster vitality, enthusiasm, even passion for the job we perform.

At eighty, when asked for the secret of happiness, the English sculptor Henry Moore said: "Have a task, something you devote your entire life to, something you bring everything to, every minute of the day for your whole life. And the most important thing is—it must be something you cannot possibly do." Hold onto that challenge and it will inspire you daily. What will endure is the imprint you leave upon your students, and their appreciation, whether expressed or not, of how you have affected their lives. Today, for example, I dropped off my son on his first day of high school and discovered that his health science teacher was a former student of mine. I suppose that should have made me feel old, but instead I felt gratified and not a little thankful. When she was in my class, I couldn't possibly have known that she would be instructing my son a decade later. But now, here she is, shaping his life—and the lives of all her students—in still unseen ways. What I passed along to her, she will pass to others, a legacy that few occupations can claim.

Continue to give thanks for the extraordinary opportunity you have every day. To each of us is given a unique identity and a realm of responsibility. What we say in the classroom—and most important, how we say it—can make a difference for years to come.

Adopt a methodical, unharried approach to your work. Use humor: it reassures people and helps them to relax. Take risks. Think out loud with your students. Let them see your mind at work. Take your work seriously, but always keep in your heart the words of G. K. Chesterton: "Angels can fly because they can take themselves lightly."

And above all, never lose touch with your inner self.

Warm regards,

CONCLUSION

During the five years that it has taken me to write these sixteen letters "to" Kelly, I've resisted many times the temptation to visit her grave. But with my work completed, I felt it was necessary to drive from my home to the Forest Lawn Mortuary, a mere seven miles away, and to stand as I'm now standing, beneath a beautiful, delicately hued sky, for a few minutes of thought.

How quickly time has slipped away. Except for the seasonal greeting card, I had fallen out of touch with her parents, and I regret that. Each year since Kelly's death her mother had sent me a warm message ending with the words, "Come see us anytime." But for reasons I can't explain, I never did. Now, both of her parents are also gone, buried here on either side of their daughter.

Had death not cut short my acquaintance with Kelly, would it have evolved into a friendship of equals? I would like to think so. The "what-ifs" abound. What if she had left home five minutes later? What if the driver of the other car had slept late that day? What if we had scheduled our meeting for a different time? But we can't play this game for long—or else we could go mad. There are no answers. Seeming blind chance strikes in all kinds of ways. "The past is a foreign country," says L. P. Hartley; "they do things differently there." It cannot be altered.

What can be changed, however, is how we think about the past and use its lessons. Kelly's death was not only a great misfortune but also a defining moment for me. I think for the first time in my life as a teacher, and I had been at it for only five years, I realized in the weeks that followed that I wasn't in the classroom for myself. I was and remain there for the students, all of whom are giving me three hours a week of their most precious possession—their time. What I say and do should make a difference in their lives. The worst thief is a bad teacher.

So why do I teach? It's my favorite question. I teach because I have an innate need to teach. I teach because I love to learn. I teach because I want to connect with people's minds and hearts at the deepest levels possible. I teach because I'm passionate about my subjects. I teach because I want to make full use of my allotted time. I teach because since childhood I have felt most comfortable on a campus, in a classroom, with books and pens and paper. I teach because it gives me a forum and the freedom to confront many of the lies and distortions that threaten to sweep modern civilization under the rug of history. I teach because I want to think as fast as possible, in as complex a way as possible, and put my thinking into forms that will perhaps benefit my students and anyone else who will listen. I teach because I need to take risks. I teach because I know that to stop teaching would be a form of self-destruction.

My father, during his youth in the early 1930s, had a recurring dream. He found himself standing at the edge of a deep ravine. A narrow walkway led to the other side, and although he wanted to cross it, he was afraid to try because far below a body lay, and he felt responsible for it being there, but he didn't know why.

We talked about this dream many times, and he told me how, as a high school student, he eventually came to understand that in his dream the body was his own—and that his fear of it kept him from walking across. At the deepest and subtlest level of his being, that body stood for some of humanity's basic fears: the fear of failure, the fear of being insignificant, and the feeling of worthlessness that comes with doubt about oneself. Not until he heard and chose to believe the words of a teacher, who said, "Accept any challenge," did my father find the courage to walk across to the other side.

Along with everything else, I believe that the role of a teacher in a student's life is to help him or her to walk across—to the other side where lies the potential to do great things and think great thoughts. The alternative—a life not lived—is unimaginable. Though Kelly didn't live to realize her potential as a teacher, my experience of knowing her and thousands of students like her continues to inspire me every day.

Finally, I teach because it gives me great joy to do so. One night over dinner I asked my mother, now eighty-five, what music means to her. She could well have had teachers in mind when she said: "It means everything to me. It's therapy. It's pleasure. It puts me into another world. It's the accomplishment. Something you can do by yourself. It works on the imagination. It's a deep feeling. Music reaches so deep that I can't explain it." Teaching and learning touch me in just such a way.

My joy that comes from this profession has sustained me through all kinds of challenges. It is a safe haven to which I can retreat and from which I emerge emboldened and clarified and confident—and very thankful.

ACKNOWLEDGMENTS

Many of the ideas in this book were nourished in conversations with my remarkable parents over a lifetime; and there isn't a page here that hasn't benefited from the fine ear and keen mind of my mother, Frances H. Salwak. I also owe a special debt of gratitude to Samuel Lee, dean of Language Arts, and Rudy Saldaña for their careful work with the manuscript and for their invaluable comments; to the selection committee, Board of Trustees, and Dr. Michael J. Viera, president of Citrus College, for granting me a sabbatical leave in the spring of 2006 that enabled me to complete the final draft of the manuscript; to Dr. Laura Nagy, my unofficial editor for twenty-five years, whose enthusiasm, loyalty, friendship, and substantive suggestions are greatly appreciated; to Jay Parini, who took time from his own work to give this effort of mine his detailed attention; to Kinn McIntosh, Ryan Salwak, and Sarah Webster for their help with the title; and to my wife, Patricia, whose exemplary life as a teacher continues to inspire me. I am equally fortunate to have the care and enthusiasm of everyone at the University of Iowa Press, all of whom have been an indispensable part of the process of getting this book into shape; and I cannot say enough for Jessie Dolch, copy editor supreme, whose conscientiousness and clear-eyed precision have made this a better book than it would have been without her contributions. This project would not have been conceivable, however, without the thousands of students I have been privileged to work with since 1973 when I began my career. In some instances, to ensure their privacy and to protect their anonymity, while preserving their stories, names and other identifying details have been changed.

Grateful acknowledgment is made for permission to reproduce the following copyrighted material:

Kingsley Amis to Dale Salwak (letter), October 10, 1990, published by HarperCollins. Reprinted by permission of the publishers and the Estate of Kingsley Amis.

W. H. Auden, "SEXT," published by Random House. Reprinted by permission of the publishers and the Estate of W. H. Auden.

Philip Larkin, "Long Lion Days," published by Faber and Faber. Reprinted by permission of the publishers and the Estate of Philip Larkin.

I am also grateful for the opportunities I had to try out some of my ideas at the Philip Larkin Society, the Modern Language Association Annual Convention, and the Barbara Pym Society North American Conference. Earlier articles or chapters in which some degree of overlap with the present book may be discerned are: "Kingsley Amis: Mimic and Moralist," *Interviews with Britain's Angry Young Men* (San Bernardino, CA: Borgo Press, 1984); "Time, Students, the Classroom and Me," *Inside English* (May 1995); "Discovering Kingsley Amis," *The Literary Biography: Problems and Solutions* (London: Macmillan; Iowa City: University of Iowa Press, 1996); "Lecturing: The Craft and the Calling," *Inside English* (May 1995); "The Sabbatical's Value: To Refresh the Mind and the Spirit," *Inside English* (March 1997); "Philip Larkin—An American View," *Biography* 21 (1998) and *About Larkin #5* (1998); "Encountering Philip Larkin," *A Passion for Books* (London: Macmillan; New York: St. Martin's, 1999); "Conclusion: A Perilous Art," *Living with a Writer* (London: Palgrave Macmillan, 2004); and "Under the Spell of Barbara Pym," *The Barbara Pym Newsletter* 11 (2005).

INDEX